Labor at the Rubicon

Labor
at the Rubicon

by J. B. S. Hardman

WITH THE EDITORIAL COLLABORATION OF

Virginia M. Hardman

New York University Press

1972

CONTENTS

INTRODUCTORY NOTE

Any analysis of the course of labor unionism in the evolving pattern of mid-twentieth century American society cannot help taking into account, if it is to remain valid, that a worldwide revolutionary upheaval is in progress and that the U.S.A. is an active part of the world. The dashing to and fro of people aboard a rapidly moving train is not an independent determinant of the train's direction. The play of forces in American society under such circumstances 'seeks its level' rather than follows 'fixed rules of the game.' . . . all this as war and peace battle for a hold on history, and as all power groups in the world, and within American society, test their strength and seek out avenues of advance.

It is 20 years since J. B. S. Hardman wrote these words in *The House of Labor* (Prentice-Hall, Inc., New York, 1951; reissued by Greenwood Press, Westport, Conn., 1970). In 1972, looking back at the last two decades, events appear to have borne out Hardman's analyses and forecasts.

At his death in 1968, Hardman was working on the problems of labor leadership and internal union democracy, a study he had begun some 15 years earlier with a Rockefeller Foundation grant and on which he continued to work long after the grant expired. *Labor at the Rubicon* is based on some of this previously unpublished material.

Postscripts at the back of the book include "What I Have Learned" (from one of the author's last manuscripts, written as part of an unpublished memoir), footnotes, and data bearing on the book's central thesis.

Appreciation is expressed to Helene Pleasants for invaluable aid in reading the final manuscript and to Prof. Emanuel Stein and Stephen C. Vladeck for generous help in seeing the book through to publication.

Remaining manuscripts and all of the Hardman papers have been acquired by Tamiment Institute Library of New York University, which will be responsible for any future publication of the Hardman material.

—V.M. Hardman

Labor at the Rubicon

A CRISIS OF CULTURE

Unequal creatures are we,
Having equal worth by birth.

On the eve of the seventies, as the poverty of affluence and poverty within affluence become ever more harshly defined and the rage against reason more pronounced, and as technological advance ever more swiftly outpaces social progress, threatening to destroy existing institutions without offering viable substitutes for them, the power of unionism as a determinant factor in the fateful outcome continues to be ignored; but is not therefore lessened. True, there are more university courses on labor and more workers' education courses on college-level subjects than ever before. But the gap between intellectuals and unionists is great and growing. Neither the unions nor the universities have yet come to a realization of their joint interest in the future of democratic processes. Given the critical American setting, that realization cannot be long delayed.

Although a minority (one-fourth) of workers in the United States are union members and a minority (slightly over one-fourth) of young people are college or university students, these multi-million minorities significantly modify American lifeways through their influence on nonunion workers and noncollege youth. Together, workers and students could be a major force for an urgently needed overhaul of America's social institutions.

In various campus upsets, students have generously helped themselves to union-developed weapons, such as strikes, sit-ins, picket lines. But they have yet to develop methods for responsible collective bargaining of negotiable issues, indeed even to spell out truly remedial proposals for real grievances. This is quite different from the terror tactics of "unnegotiable demands"; while immediate returns may seem rewarding, the final pay-off promises to be rather unpleasant. For the Right is being even more swiftly "radicalized" than the student transients of the New Left, and the cutting edge of its backlash may soon be felt in the land.

An alternative prospect, and one that could effectively counter the radical right, is a new union-university rapprochement, of the kind that enlisted in the old days the understanding help of such rich personalities as John Dewey and Paul Douglas, to name only two of the many intellectual stalwarts who made the union struggle for a decent life their own and which, in the thirties, reached a high point from which there has been a continuing decrescendo. Today too many union members dismiss student activists as the children of affluence playing at revolution; and too many students dismiss the union members as middle-class defenders of the Establishment. Both need to know each other better.

In the current shakeup of American values presaging broad institutional change, the labor movement has a vital concern in the sociopolitical and intellectual complexion of the generation that will soon be taking over. And the nation's youth, in turn, can ill afford continued alienation from the union movement which is its strongest and in fact only potential ally. Mutual understanding in depth, on the part of unionism and the universitites, is demanded by their common stake in the survival of intelligence and democratic processes in this twilight of a civilization.

That common stake overrides the failings of some individual union leaders and practices as it overrides the shortcomings of some student leaders and their tactics.

Union in the Labor Community

The term labor, as used in these studies, includes union members, officers and organizations; paid professionals and technicians on union staffs; and also outside pro-labor consultants who have chosen to identify themselves with the trade union movement.

Thousands of professionals and intellectuals, some fairly prominent and some unknown, help widen the union movement's horizons.

Regardless of the specific activities of individual unions and their leaders, the aggregate called labor is an entity with an ever-broadening role in the making of American history. Already established as an integral part of the nation's socioeconomic fabric, the technological transformation of American life is now quickening labor's political pulse.

Earlier than any other segment of the population, perhaps because it is more immediately affected, labor has grasped the implications of the change-over from an industrialized to a computerized society. Labor is keenly aware of the fact that, no matter how radical the transformation of lifeways, including the nature and meaning of work itself that has resulted from accelerating cybernation, automation, computerization, and their complex concomitants, what matters most is man himself. Without that central core of the human species, there is nothing, a detail sometimes overlooked by the master planners of research and development. Labor has lived dangerously for so long that even in these "affluent" times it senses the political pitfalls inherent in the socioeconomic lag created by a runaway technology.

In a democratic society such as ours still is, labor has political weight, comprising as it does over twenty million unionists who, in effect, are a cohesive mechanism of the most numerous segment of the adult population. There are eighteen million active union members and about two million retirees maintaining close ties with the unions. These twenty million have a broad influence on their families and friends and also, and most importantly, on more than sixty million nonunion members of the national work force. [In 1970 there were 20.7 million unionists.]

Unions, of course, differ in many ways, on a basis of skills and trades, of blue or white-collar type of employment, and also due to regional, ethnic, and cultural factors which color political predispositions. But variegated as they are, the unions nonetheless comprise a well-cemented entity. All are labor. All adhere, in greater or lesser degree, to a conduct implicit in the logic of their economic positions. All accept and abide by the mandatory common law of unionism, a shared commitment to solidarity. that is buttressed by binding constitutions, by-laws, and enforcement machinery.

/ The strength of the unions, multiplied by their impact on the numerically larger non-union sector of the work force, has created a power reservoir placing unionism in the forefront of the nation's social forces./True, organized labor's influence on the unorganized workers is not continuous nor always sharply evident. But its reality is tellingly demonstrated in crisis situations, as when unorganized workers respond en masse, sometimes by the tens of thousands, to strike calls issued by relatively small unions. Outstanding examples include the 1902 strike of anthracite coal miners; the steel workers' strikes of 1892, 1908 and 1919; and the 1934 textile strike. The 1919 steel strike was called by a union with less than 10,000 members; close to 400,000 steel workers responded in the decisive struggle against a most powerful combine of immensely rich and ruthless employers. Nor are these isolated cases. They constitute in large part the story of how unions are built. This is how the automobile and needle trades were organized. And it is how service and white-collar workers (insofar as they are being organized) are being drawn into the trade unions. Without this dynamic impingement of the organized minority on the unorganized majority, the labor movement inevitably tends to stagnate.

The general public also has been enlisted in a variety of union-initiated actions. For example, the consumer boycott of California grapes in the late 1960s was effectively supported by persons having no connection with labor but who felt that the pickers had a right to organize for a living wage. And if a guaranteed annual income is enacted into law in the seventies, it will be due in no small part to labor initiatives in the 1960s. Looking back for a moment, it was the unions who aroused public interest in the historic cases of Sacco and Vanzetti and of Tom Mooney. Unionists and the general public have similarly made common cause in a number of less-celebrated efforts for social justice and civil rights.

The union movement's influence on legislation has had an effect on the quality of life for all Americans. Labor has been in the forefront of virtually every effort for social and economic advance in the nation from free compulsory education in the early days of the Republic to the legal decisions in our time to safeguard voting rights of all Americans, and to desegregate schools and end all forms of racial discrimination. (This is not to deny or ignore the discriminatory practices of the construction trades and some other unions where ugly anti-Negro attitudes still prevail. On this score, labor's first order of business is to clean its own house of any and every element of remaining racism.) Job-safety regulations, child-labor laws, unemployment insurance, Medicare, Medicaid, and the basic Social Security program, including the ongoing effort for more adequate coverage, owe much to union vision and pressure. As an integral part of American society, labor obviously does not live in a vacuum but in mutual interdependence with other large social entities which it affects and is affected by. As labor contributes to and shares in the nation's progress, so too it bears the scars of every act of national backwardness and dishonor.

*   *   *

The cause of labor's current and continuing malady was traced to its proper source almost ten years ago when Walter P. Reuther, President of the United Automobile Workers, said: "Labor is in trouble because America is in trouble." This was true in the 1950s and the sixties; nor is there any prospect of abatement in the 1970s. The forecast is for stormier weather ahead as the unresolved crises of almost a quarter of a century press for solution. Unfortunately Reuther's cogent summing up of the actuality situation still prevails.

Doubtless there have been worse times, but none meaner. Material, spiritual and mental corruption have come to be widely accepted as an unpleasant but necessary component of bigness. Words, like people, appear to have ever-diminishing value; an inflated rhetoric produces such absurdities as "negative growth" to define what was once called depression. Truth and trust are shaken to their foundations. Against a background of accelerating social dissolution, today's most urgent need may well be the search for pragmatic solutions and truths on which groups and individuals can base new relationships as the foundation of a genuine human solidarity. History's assignment to the present college generation may well be that fundamental task. In this effort to find, recognize, and nurture the human element, the American trade union movement has a wealth of experience on which to build, a pragmatic knowledge shared by no other sector of society.

Unfortunately a large segment of the public appears to believe that the unions now constitute enormous power blocs pursuing their own selfish ends without restraint and regardless of the public interest. There is a widespread notion that workers are wallowing in ever greater abundance, that they have seized far more than their due share of the economic pie. This is of course a crude misreading of the balance sheet of power distribution in our society. True, labor is stronger than it ever has been, but it certainly cannot settle all disputes on its own terms. It has a long way to go before it can, if ever, relax its guard.

The fact is that continuing inflation each year devours wage gains won at the bargaining table. The result is that real wages have tended to be almost static while prices rise. The free-enterprise system is losing its first, essential qualifying adjective, the one on which consumer-workers depend in order to be able to pay bills. Some two decades past the midcentury mark, labor's share of increased productivity has been far outpaced by management's soaring profits. Nor can the uneasy marriage of convenience between the AFL and CIO offer much protection. That alliance of not-too-ardent partners is shakier than it has ever been. Employers, meanwhile, have increasingly consolidated their business enterprises; vast, diversified conglomerates, many worldwide, have given management a solid base for maintaining employer prerogatives and fighting back against increased labor demands. At the end of the sixties the competition supposedly and once in fact characteristic of the free-enterprise system was fast disappearing, with no less than two-thirds of the nation's manufacturing assets owned by only 200 firms.

In contrast, the unions and unionists, despite their much-touted affluence and power, are at no time secure in their freedom and rights in the work places. They must forever garner and husband their socioeconomic strength, safeguarding their political equality with management in the federal and state legislative and law-enforcement establishments. Labor now, as always, shares the uncertainties of democracy itself.

Today, as a result of industry consolidation and concentration, prices can go up even when the demand goes down. What happens then to economics and the consumer is anybody's guess. But where the major onus lies is clear—with management and its illegal price-fixing activities. And the remedy? A new injection of freedom into the enterprise system, a new assumption of public responsibility to rectify industry's irresponsibilities, an end to built-in obsolescence and wasteful, deceptive packaging, and a new orientation of the economy for the fulfillment of human needs rather than for corporate greed. This would in part require only implementing existing legislation and statutes, such as the antitrust laws, and reformation of the tax structure. It would also require the evolution of new concepts and of a legal framework for transforming an economy of waste into an economy geared to human and environmental needs. This is a large order, but it is the order of the day. It is the direction in which labor is moving. Its drive for a whole spectrum of expanding fringe benefits has created the possibility of a protective umbrella for all Americans against the hazards of age, disability, ill health, unemployment, and structural poverty. True, our rudimentary social security and health and welfare programs leave much to be desired, but a beginning has been made. Labor's effort to put more muscle into the embryonic "welfare state" essentially postulates the continued existence of the free private-enterprise system. No social radicalism underlines American laborism. Dominated largely by conservative leaders, with a membership whose aspirations are predominantly middle class, the union movement has never been in serious discord with the existing social structure.

But it cannot therefore be assumed that unions are unconditionally loyal to the profit-motive system. No union of workers employed in the TVA enterprises has yet expressed a yearning to turn the giant power complex over to private ownership.

Revolution Minus Barricades

Despite their conservative instincts, or perhaps due to them, the unions have exerted a revolutionizing influence on American life. This should be evident to anyone capable of discerning the long-term consequences of seemingly small events and of discriminating between what is real and what is readily visible.

Although the word "revolution" commonly connotes barricades and terrorism, some of the most enduring revolutions have dispensed with both. And of course the alleged beneficiaries of the bloody revolutions on record, the common men or masses, have rarely been greatly rewarded for their efforts. The hellish realities of Thermidor have always been more convincingly materialized than the pre-revolutionary promises of heaven on earth. The long-term meaning of a specific revolution is of necessity beyond the knowledge of the participants. But within a restricted definition of the term, as identifying essential changes in the social power structure of a nation, labor has indeed been a revolutionizing force in American society, transforming individual lives and the whole fabric of socioeconomic and political relationships.

Thus in the 1930s an employee of the U.S. Steel Corporation lived in an America vastly different from the America of today, the America which his union helped shape. In the old days a steelworker had no job security, no voice in setting pay or work hours and conditions, and no protection against age, ill health or disability. The corporation paid retired workers an overall pension of some 70 dollars a year. The first payment was usually accompanied by a letter wishing the retiree "a long and happy tirement" on 5.84 dollars a month. (Nor were these "benefits" provided by U.S. Steel an exception to the prevailing practice in the industry.) Within one generation, a radical transformation had been achieved. The going had not been easy; it was marked by strife, strikes, and bloodshed. But by 1950 the same steelworker, employed by the same U.S. Steel Corporation, was a member of a powerful union that protected his job, terms of employment, paid holidays and vacations. Today's steelworker has substantial fringe benefits, including health, unemployment and life insurance. Before the end of the 1960s company-paid pension benefits were 5 dollars a month for each year of service. Those forced to retire as a result of plant shutdowns, prolonged layoffs or disability were receiving a 75 dollars per month supplement to regular pension benefits until eligible for social security. In 1968 over 100,000 retired steelworkers were receiving pension payments from industry's insurance fund.

The steel workers are a politically alert group, active and respected in their communities. Their union, the United Steelworkers of America, ranks high in the union world both for what it has achieved for its more than 1,100,000 members and for its constructive, intelligent role in the life of the nation and of the localities where its members live and work.

The comparatively small Federation of Musicians also won a revolution without barricades. Faced with the steady decline of employment for musicians, the Federation in 1942 finally succeeded, after many attempts, in imposing a protective tax or royalty on recordings. The tax funds enabled the union to organize free public concerts employing live musicians and to support unemployed members, thus keeping the profession alive despite the inroads of the record business. But because of these activities, the union was accused of seeking to undermine free private enterprise and was sued in the courts. Union president James Caesar Petrillo disclaimed any political intent, let alone revolutionary goals, saying: "We are just interested in musicians and musicians only."

Petrillo was a staid, conservative union leader, with no interest whatsoever in *zukunft* music, but circumstances compelled him to perform the role of a seemingly radical leader, a not altogether unusual phenomenon in history.

Events forced an even more revolutionary role on that staunch Republican and loyalist of free enterprise, John L. Lewis. Again, it was not choice or ideology but crude circumstance that determined the radical quality of the Lewis leadership which, with the power of an elemental force that also knows every trick in the book, transformed the life of the miners, engineering a monumental advance for human decency in one of the most brutal of twentieth-century industries. Within the memory of living miners, coal mining meant a life of grinding poverty and catastrophe, characterized by early death, widespread disease and disability. As Lewis told a Senate subcommittee on safety, bituminous and anthracite operations between 1920 and 1950 took a toll of 20,397 miners killed. In 1951 alone, 800 men lost their lives in accidents. Others were totally or partially incapacitated, some burned beyond recognition, some deprived of sight, limbs, mobility. There were the debilitating, often killing lung diseases, which have yet to be brought under control. And to compound the anguish of the mining towns came mechanization and the competition of other fuels.

Yet Lewis's demand for a royalty on every ton of coal mined was attacked even more harshly than the musicians' demand for a royalty on recordings. It was denounced as a "Bolshevik revolution" and made no headway when first put forward in 1945; a year later it was part of the contract. The employers originally paid 5 cents on each ton of coal mined, and this was gradually increased to 40 cents. The revolutionizing quality of the achievement is indicated by the following facts and figures. By 1955 the United Mine Workers of America's Welfare and Retirement Fund had collected from employers close to one billion dollars in royalties. (This covers only soft-coal miners and does not include similar payments to the anthracite coal division of the union.) Of that total some 900 million dollars went for various forms of compensation and protection of miners and their families. As of June 30, 1955, there were 59,482 miners receiving pensions of 100 dollars per month from the fund in addition to medical and other benefits. Pensions have since been substantially increased.[1]

The UMWA Fund for many years operated its own modern, well-equipped hospitals which restored large numbers of men to health and useful activity. The American Medical Association denounced the venture as socialized medicine. With shrinkage of the industry, the hospitals were sold, but excellent medical and surgical care continues to be provided through The Medical, Health and Hospital Service of the Fund. The organization arranges and pays for a broad scope of services to nearly half a million beneficiaries by 7240 physicians in 1,730 hospitals, medical, research, and special centers.

When Lewis announced his retirement in 1960 after forty years as the mine workers leader, one grief-stricken worker was quoted by United Press as saying: "When I started in the mines, my hourly pay rate was 13 cents. Now I get $24 a day. Lewis did this for us."

Of course many miners lost their jobs, for Lewis gave man-

agement an almost free hand in automation. Between 1920 and
1960 two-thirds of the mining jobs were cut. In 1948 there were
some 400,000 miners; in 1960 about 200,000 were employed. But
miners can retire at age 55 on full pension and the industry was
enabled to survive serious troubles when coal lost ground as a
competitive fuel.

It was Lewis who earlier had urged the captains of the coal
industry "to behave like capitalists." Faced with industry and
employment contraction, this "revolutionary" Republican taught
free enterprise the art of enterprising so that a sick industry
could modernize, function, succeed.

The mineworkers, musicians and steelworkers are part of a
large and largely varied story in which the Auto Workers with
Walter Reuther and of course the needle trades with David Dubinsky and Sidney Hillman played major, well-known roles, in-
dicating the scope of a revolution achieved by the prosaic
collaterals of the union performance in America.

/ Old age security, paid vacations, coffee breaks, union health
centers, educational training, and other fringe benefits mark a
telling change in lifeways and status for millions of workers.
From being degraded "hands" without vote, voice, or protection
in their work and daily lives, they have become respected citizens
with human dignity and the power to protect themselves. Management no longer can determine wages and working conditions
unilaterally, but must submit their determination to collective
bargaining sessions which recognize the legitimate equity rights
of workers in their jobs and skills. This unrevolutionary revolution has not produced instant paradise, but it has removed labor
quite a distance from hell. More than 50 years after the Bolshevik
take-over, the common men of the Russian Revolution, not the
commissars and managers, would doubtless happily "settle" for
50 percent of the American unionized workers' take-home pay,
benefits, and freedoms. /

The Honey and the Sting

From the thirties on through and immediately after the war
years, American labor moved fast, often crowding a decade's

progress into a year, building and utilizing social power, developing labor institutionalism as a recognized part of American democratic society. Proceeding with gusto, most of the time without preconceived plans, labor's pragmatic approach to central issues is helping shape national history. This assessment of labor's contribution to the social mainstream is not invalidated by some of the ugly facts of union life, such as pockets of corruption, patches of racism, and faulty operation of the democratic process in some unions. These evils exist. They do not predominate. Nor do unions have a monopoly on what the U.S. Senate Committee's Permanent Investigations Subcommittee [2] euphemistically referred to as malpractice. For its investigations revealed that management was honeycombed with the most malodorous malpractices, performed, of course, under the enlightened guidance of high-priced protecting counsel. Despite the McClellan Committee disclosures, management did nothing to clean house; it merely sought to improve its public relations "image." Labor's high command, in contrast, cooperated with the Senate Committee, expelled its biggest union, the 1,400,000-member Teamsters, suspended others found guilty of corrupt activities, and adopted a code of ethical practices.

Unions, unlike management, moreover, have no power of selection; they must take their members as they find them in the work places, without regard to character or quality. And in the unions, as elsewhere, brave souls are not cheaper by the dozen but rather in short supply. Not unlike professors, clergymen, congressmen or merchants, unionists prefer to play safe. Nor does virtue always rule, even in situations where the good and true are numerically preponderant. For nowhere do majorities actually govern. In labor, as everywhere, active, articulate minorities contend for power. The ideas they project may be good, evil, or somewhere in between. Each seeks acceptance by the majority, and the minority that wins "writes the ticket." The union movement was fortunate in the critical thirties, and again in the fifties and sixties in that the more enlightened minorities generally prevailed. In consequence labor today is a positive force for social advance. But unions live in the nation and are influenced by the very environment they seek to alter.

America in Trouble

Never has so affluent a society exhibited such mounting anxiety as America since the mid-fifties. True, the affluence is far from universal. The tensions, however, are real.

"Enjoy! Enjoy!" seems to have become the battle hymn of the Republic with a soaring leisure boom threatening to catch up with and surpass even defense expenditures. As early as 1954, *Fortune* magazine estimated the leisure and recreation market at 30.6 billion dollars. The "fun market" has since just about tripled.[3]

Not everyone, of course, is affluent; not the working poor, not the unemployed. One-fifth of this phenomenally productive nation is impoverished. Some are too old or too young or too unskilled to get jobs. But one-third of the poor are heads of families with full-time jobs. These working poor number in the millions. Additional millions live on poverty's grim borderlines. And seemingly well-paid workers see the pay raises in new contracts nibbled away by rising prices.

Unemployment rose from 3.3 percent in 1951 to 5.5 percent in 1960.[4]

In 1964 the Department of Labor reported that in an average work week "almost 3.9 million jobless sought and failed to find employment. Another 2.5 million who wanted full-time jobs could only find part-time work." We had uninterrupted prosperity from 1962 to 1968 and a continuous increase of the gross national income from 1960 to 1968 as well. But the number of jobless did not decrease until the war in Viet Nam broke the back of rising unemployment; the break was temporary. Unemployment is on the rise. We are the richest nation on earth. Our engineering talent, business competence, and trading ingenuity are second to none. Our productive capacity is unequalled. And yet we have not even begun to come to grips with the immense problem of poverty in our land, exacerbated now by galloping inflation.

As a people we live in a hiatus of enlarging social lag in which each step out of the *status quo* is swiftly outdistanced by advancing technology. Those most responsible for creating the inequities in distribution of the nation's productivity, or real wealth, are being called upon to solve the poverty problem and, not unnaturally, can not do so. And as inflation bites into the socioeconomic fabric, it is beginning to tear at the political structure. A not entirely unjustified fear prevails lest the old horses of social progress cut loose or drop dead.

Against this background, only fools can be complacent. As we approach the closing decades of the century, the union movement, like every responsible segment of society, is worried about its staying power in the stormy seventies. Labor's anxiety is indeed the expression of a healthy will to survive in a vastly complex situation. Nor is the task made easier by awareness of the inherent difficulties of adapting traditional union methods to a swiftly altering new world, which is both smaller and more divided than it has ever been.

It was outgoing President Dwight D. Eisenhower who, as early as 1960, clearly warned the nation against the industrial-military complex. That complex is still the proving ground of a militant, potentially violent reactionary combine typified by the John Birch Society. This small, tightly controlled conspiracy has its own grand design for the conquest of the United States by the know-nothings and a modernized Ku Klux Klan, with the Republican Party emblem as a concealing fig leaf.

Actually it was during Ike's own somnolent regime that the radical right prospered and developed muscle. Nor was it routed by the ensuing Kennedy and Johnson administrations. Its "literature," spokesmen and supporters extend now into nearly all segments of the national community.

In 1961 John F. Kennedy issued his inspiriting challenge, "Ask not what the country can do for you but what you can do for your country." A youthful minority responded; it was soon disenchanted by the realities of the undeclared Viet Nam war. The affluent continued "to enjoy." The radical right continued to mobilize. Albeit defeated, Barry Goldwater's "cause" gathered momentum. Senator J. William Fulbright cried out in rage against what he described as "the richest, fattest, smuggest, and most complacent people who ever failed to meet the test of survival."

In the sixties a new generation of college youth decided that the only test of survival worth meeting was that of individual conscience. Under Martin Luther King's great leadership, Negroes quickened their march toward freedom; and a sizable number of whites walked and worked with them. But expectancies outdistanced victories. Verbal war was soon declared on the Establishment, the system and all its works. The proponents of black separatism, with its racial rallying cries and stress on black studies courses, spiced with the always reliable admixture of anti-Semitism, tried to drown out the urgent need for full, meaningful integration. The black nationalists, of course, did not represent majority black opinion, nor its tested leadership. But they captured the TV screen and popular imagination. There was a new excitement, thrust, and vocabulary for those who were understandably impatient with the slow, cumbersome, often unresponsive legal steps towards integration. Stokely Carmichael was not shy in spelling out his goal as the destruction of the United States: "We don't want peace in Vietnam! We want the Vietnamese to defeat the United States of America," in *The New York Times* (December 7, 1967). Most of the old leadership was forced to quicken its step and sharpen its rhetoric in competing with the new, more radical leaders. At the same time such organizations as the NAACP and leaders such as Roy Wilkins continued their fundamental work of enlarging freedom and full citizenship rights for Negroes. Meanwhile the young white activists, deprived of their former leadership roles in the Negro integration movement, focused more and more on the unending Viet Nam war. Draft evasion gave way to draft denunciation and to ever-widening protest against the war, its leaders and finally against a system of government that could not or would not get out of Viet Nam. Some of the white militants clung to the fringes and were tolerated at the periphery of the Black Power movement. The first demonstrations were on the campuses, obviously the most vulnerable of the Establishment institutions. But in the process of trying to destroy the universities, the New Left fed new life into the Old Right.

Looking back briefly at the 1950s and 1960s, however, not all intelligence and decency vanished. Although the number of delinquents, criminals, and irresponsibles increased, they did not dominate the scene. The Supreme Court outlawed segregation in public schools and public places even though desegregation still moves at no more than a turtle's pace. The Voting Rights Act was passed. The Bill of Rights is still with us; it may be bruised and dented, but as yet it has not been junked. Negroes are increasingly being elected to public office and are securing entrance into universities, industries, and professions once closed to them. The need is for prompt, widespread acceleration; there is little travel time left for the fulfillment of overdue promissory notes.

There may be no happy end to the seventies. But the undertaker is not at the door. Nor is the United States at all ready to lie down in the grave which Nikita Krushchev's successors have been busily readying.

The 1950s (in the face of McCarthyism, the Korean War, the Cold War and the development of the H-bomb) illustrated the dangers of nonengagement; the confrontations of the 1960s (in the face of the Southeast Asia and the Middle East conflicts, the widening gaps between rich and poor, between black and white, old and young, computerization and human needs) illustrated the dangers of resorting to moral fanaticism to solve complex socioeconomic and political problems.

As the decade moved to a close and the unhappy war in Viet Nam took its unending course and toll, we became an ever more fragmented nation, unsure of ourselves, distrusting each other. This dangerous period of transition cannot be indefinitely prolonged. No culture can long survive in a state of stasis, merely by paying sporadic blackmail to its most threatening factions. Ultimately the price of internal peace cannot thus be met. But the habits of the market place die hard. We have yet to learn that we cannot fulfill the Supreme Court mandates for full integration by buying off dissenters, rioters, and rabble rousers. Nor will wishful screams and pious statements end the Viet Nam war. We have to recognize that all the research and development departments in the world cannot produce the blueprints for a viable culture. Neither, of course, will such slogans as Power to the People, and Off the Pigs.

In the old days labor often served as a catalyst for social change. It must do so again, and in ever larger degree. We have the means to end poverty and exploitation. We are the first great nation that can actually afford to harness the immense power of automation for human welfare, rather than for individual aggrandizement. What we seem to lack is a cohesive will.

The exploitation of human and natural resources for private profit must be brought under control so that it ceases to damage the general interest and begins to advance it. To do so we must move towards the start of a production-for-individual-development democracy on a scale never before attempted. The contours of the future are uncertain. They need not be fearful.

With reason tempered by compassion, a sense of social responsibility, and a due awareness of man's infinite fallibility, we may begin to lose that fatal sense of moral righteousness now rending the nation apart and develop a sense of community, of national direction.

Great Expectations and Great Dangers

"If there is great danger," President Johnson said in his State of the Union message on January 4, 1965, "there is now also the excitement of great expectations."

Never burdened by an undue sense of modesty, Johnson had obviously decided that he would go down in history as the creator of the Great Society. As a politician, he naturally did not intend to get there in seven-league boots. Nor did many in the august assembly favor so swift a pace of locomotion. The "great expectations" were long range and would be fulfilled by the law of detours. As to "the great danger," that was clear and present enough; it is still with us, and ever-enlarging.

The main threat is not the continuing possibility of global nuclear war. Only the U.S.A. and the U.S.S.R. could wage that lethal, half-hour conflict, and neither wants a war that would destroy both. China talks big, but cup and lip are still apart. Responsible communist strategists incline toward the nibbling method of infiltration and subversion to "bury capitalism." The going is slower, but it costs less in money and manpower, and there is no risk of direct retaliation. For the free world still has inhibitions about countering subversion and guerrilla warfare with all-out war. Until free peoples learn an effective way of controlling these so-called "small wars," they will continue to be the preferred method of communist aggression.

The crux of our grave danger is neither the "advisory" war in Southeast Asia nor the lend-lease, of sorts, of war tools to friendly dictators in Africa and elsewhere, although on balance these commitments add up to plague the nation materially and morally.

Our paramount danger is domestic. It is the lack of intellectual stamina, evident both in the self-protective withdrawal into isolationism and in the self-destructive rage of unreason. True, the Enlightenment, which more or less held thinking men together for some two centuries, destroyed its last credentials in the Nazi and Communist holocausts of our time. The events of this century alone have demonstrated how narrow is the cul-de-sac into which pure reason can lead. Surely no one can now dispute that while man without reason is nothing, man with reason alone is less than nothing. Not only the old religious and ideological concepts have been shattered, but the new faith in science has become properly suspect.

The nonengaged and the much-engaged fanatics are alike in their basic repudiation of reason. A widespread feeling of distrust of self, of the community, and the nation further prevents the kind of meaningful communication among reasonable men on which our very lives depend. The astronauts whose performances and very survival require communication between space and earth illustrate the kind of vital interchange (quite different from popular "dialogues") without which the human species cannot much longer cling to the evolutionary ladder.

We live at a time when vocal minorities, claiming moral superiority, rely increasingly on force to achieve spurious victories. And an apathetic, mute majority seems incapable of movement until shoved with force by determined militants of the right and left. Meanwhile, an intellectual and moral inflation has created a rhetoric devoid of value.

Jean Jacques Rousseau, whose ideas had a powerful impact on American Revolutionary thinking, considered democracy to be a permanent, ongoing revolution. Inaction, paralysis of the spirit, are latter-day developments representing the true degradation of democratic principles. There are many contributing causes. But the roots of the evil can be traced to World War II. Today's youth are predominantly war babies, and they hate the war they see on their TV's. They are determined to stop it. Today's parents are, in large numbers, war returnees; they, too, watch the TV; but live by trying to keep out of trouble.

As a result, national cohesion is fragmented. Americans appear bewildered by the apparent loss of their once characteristic urge to move on, try the unknown, reach for the stars.

America's trouble is not primarily economic or political. It is the lack of a concerted "we," the lack of thoughtful unity, the absence of consensus on direction. Abraham Lincoln said it in simple, telling words when he told an earlier, divided nation: "If we could first know where we are, and whither we are tending, we could better judge what to do and do it better."

At this crossing of eras when intellectual stock-taking can no longer be delayed, the difficulties are compounded by the disarray of the old radicalism and the lack of hard thinking among the new radicals. The ideas of social justice and democracy advanced by Eugene V. Debs, Morris Hillquit and Norman Thomas have not been updated; they have indeed been corrupted by the Fascists and Communists to a degree that has made the very word "ideas" suspect.

In the ensuing intellectual stasis, unionism has on the whole performed better than might have been expected, if not as well as was needed. It did not avoid engagement when required, nor did it indulge in purposeless acts of rage or violence. Its efforts, admittedly, were not always directed towards involvement in the great issues of the day, but at least they were real and steadily focused on trying to change the social power relationship in the established national structure.

Labor's trouble, like the country's, has not been so much lack of power or organization, but failure, thus far, to equate enhanced power and standing with supporting intellectual force. This is in large measure a crisis of culture. At issue is not any kind of conventional schooling or education. What is needed in labor, as in the nation, is a world outlook, a cohesive orientation, an honest assessment of the status quo and to come, and the mental strength to take on history as enemy or cooperator, as the case may be.

Unions are, above all, a phenomenon of human culture, and in the sweep of history, a very recent phenomenon at that. Whether or not their friends or enemies recognize it, unionism is part of the dynamics of modern social history, shaping and shaped by its multitudinous crises. Any valid assessment of unionism's flaws and achievements must include consideration of the frustrating tensions of our time, and the corrupting environment of national life in the 1950s and 1960s.

Concomitantly, within the unions themselves, internal pressures were contradictory; to move on with greater force from positions of strength or to rest on the oars since so much had been gained. Nor were external pressures one-directional. Management, at times, has appeared to have grown battle-weary; open fights on unionism have become rare. But efforts to halt union progress, to nibble at its power, remain almost unceasing. And every so often, as during the Kohler strike, management bared strong teeth. In the circumstances, the union movement did not stand still. But it is not unfair to ask whether, as argued by some leaders, greater advance might not have been made by greater mobility of men and ideas.

The Missing More

Labor's most pressing need now, and for the past two decades, has been for more organizing activity, more effort to bring the movement into greater consonance with the expanding exigencies of a basically revolutionary period. The suggestions that follow indicate directions for long overdue union action on a broad scale.

First, unionism's arrested numerical growth can be overcome by a larger expenditure of money and manpower designed to reach into new, still non-union areas and to close existing gaps in those that are fairly well organized. For two and a half decades there have been no great campaigns, no large-scale investment of risk capital in great organizing drives. Modest efforts have been made here and there and most of these have been modestly successful. Of course the cost of organizing a non-union worker has multiplied several times since the thirties. But developing greater unions is still the best investment for union dollars. Costs are temporary, the returns continuing.

Politically, labor has never been stronger; and the content of its sociopolitical thinking has advanced substantially from the old Gompersian line of "reward friends, punish enemies." But the overriding need is for new concepts to revitalize and invigorate the democratic process itself; to pour new functional content into some of the now moribund forms of political procedures, making them more responsive to the complex, changed and changing ways of public life and thinking. Admittedly, this is a large order. Admittedly, labor's own internal democratic procedures would profit by such reexamination and reinforcement, which would strengthen labor and also open new avenues of approach to the solution of critical national issues. Labor has made no secret of its displeasure with the way things are. And it has made some tangible proposals for improvements. But it could and should do more probing beneath the surface.

To date there has been no maximal effort by organized labor to help solve the central problem of full Negro liberation. Some unions have done a good deal. Some unions stayed home. The overall movement has tragically failed to come to grips with this all-important issue. Labor's high command supported the basic principles involved in breaking the barriers to Negro entry into the economic mainstream of American life. But what is needed are results. And time is running out. Large goals require large means. And if labor does not undertake this task, who will? What is needed is an all-out, concentrated, expertly conceived and conducted drive to open the doors to full and equal participation for Negroes within the union movement.

The national union movement can and should designate a multimillion dollar Negro Labor Campaign Fund and promptly place in the field several hundred black and white expert organizers for a massive drive to unionize Negro workers, employed and unemployed. The most knowledgeable, skilled organizers of the various national unions should be used for this effort in strategic, selected areas across the country. This national drive must be coordinated with auxiliary organizations for job training and placement, as part of the war on poverty. It must be done on a large scale because nothing less will do. And concomitantly, the last vestiges of racism must be swept out of labor's own house. This proposal is not a sidewalk superintendent's phantasy. It was, in effect, the pattern of action used by John L. Lewis and his associates of the CIO in 1936 when they launched the powerful campaign to unionize the unorganized steel, rubber, textile, and other great industries.

A drive with teeth in it for full Negro economic rights through union organization would make real impact in this major crisis area. It would mean tangible results in the reduction of poverty, fear, violence, and an increase of purposiveness, unity, and individual dignity. As a fringe benefit, such a drive might capture the imagination of many of our alienated youth and enlist their useful participation. An inter-color solidaristic union organizing campaign could measurably undercut the slogan of Black Power which, despite rationalizations and would-be "clarifications," is a call for civil war. Only positive action to cleanse the clogged arteries of the democratic system can prevent this determined, minuscule minority from achieving that goal. Black-white union solidarity on the move is an important part of the answer.

Another area of neglected opportunity that presents an immediate challenge to the unions is the organization of white-collar workers, the fastest growing segment of the labor force, and also the one facing the progressive decimation of automation. Except for the teachers, only piecemeal efforts have been made to organize these people, and the results have been far from spectacular. In 1961, however, the small Teachers Federation in New York City won, in a dramatic collective bargaining election, the votes of over thirty thousand, and their example set the pattern for Detroit, Philadelphia, and other large cities across the country. The United Federation of Teachers under the leadership of Albert Shanker, a one-time junior-high school mathematics teacher, and civil rights activist with a Socialist background, rapidly expanded in numbers and accordingly increased its demands. The union expanded so rapidly and began to disregard so many accepted taboos, apart from violating the Taylor Law, that the UFT was widely viewed, even in pro-labor circles, as highly "controversial." [5]

In 1961 the Postal Workers secured an exclusive contract;

and greater effort might yield better results than have since been attained. A major difficulty, however, is that government workers are by law denied the right to strike, although all other organized workers are guaranteed that right by law. And this is especially important because the government, on the federal, state, and local level, is the biggest and fastest growing employer of labor. A way must be found out of this discriminatory paradox. Nobody can chop wood with his hands tied behind his back; the no-strike laws tie labor's hands in the public employment field. Every so often, strikes occur anyway, in which case the unions are fined and the leaders jailed or threatened with jail sentences. Meanwhile the strike is customarily denounced as a national emergency and the workers gain a little when a new contract is agreed upon. Here, as elsewhere, legislation that fails to enlist the support of those most directly affected by it is difficult, if not impossible to enforce. Nor is anything gained by having laws on the statute books that are inevitably violated, thus adding to the general spirit of lawlessness that is contributing to the break-down of democratic processes.

In the white-collar field proper, the teachers are only one unit of a vast field in which organization is needed but is handicapped by a built-in difficulty; for the "salariat" generally considers itself socially superior to bricklayers, teamsters, and other manual, blue-collar and service workers who predominate in the unions. White-collar workers generally shy away from the word "union"; they have nonetheless a proved capacity for responding affirmatively to the actuality of the union when a more palatable nomenclature is used, such as guild or association.[6] And since stupidity is not a crime but a misfortune, it is up to labor to make the appropriate verbal adjustments. If several white-collar unions were to set up a federation or association with a prestigious enough professional label, it is not inconceivable that more of the status-conscious white-collar workers would join up. That was how the newspaper industry was organized in the thirties. There was the prestige appeal of Heywood Broun, who was not only a dedicated pro-labor man, but a famed $25,000-a-year columnist, and there was the status appeal of the word "guild" instead of union. The American Newspaper Guild is no more loved by the newspaper publishers than are the printers and truckers unions, and it is as good a union as any.

The blue-jean AFL-CIO workers would be wise to finance a white-collar movement, called by any name, even if the eggs were nominally laid in somebody else's basket. In the end a federation of labor and an association of white collarites would be doing essentially the same kind of work along much the same lines and for the same goals. Labor as a whole would be strengthened, as would the nation. Moreover, as computerization and automation are, in some sense, a bleaching process by which blue-collar jobs can be expected to fade increasingly into white-collar work, the element of enlightened self-interest is not entirely absent.

The proposals mentioned above indicate possible directions and some of the problems, pressures and counter-pressures to which the labor movement is exposed. In the end the measure of a movement's worth is in its selection of which pressures to counter and which to exert, and in how effectively it does both, remembering always that "The gods lead the wise and drag the stubborn."

A Full Day's Work

The increasing importance of labor in American democratic society has made it a matter of proper concern to virtually the entire citizenry, for the relations between labor and industry and its involvement in politics, the political operation of democracy have all changed in one generation, now that the government is the biggest employer of labor, the biggest buyer of military hardware and consumer goods, and the major investor in research. Perhaps the time has now come to apply to unionism the old saying about war and the generals: Labor is too serious a matter to be left to the labor leaders alone.

In the United States, unlike Britain, Germany, and the other democracies, the labor movement is closed to all but wage earners. Yet the unions' expanding impact on decision-making in ever widening areas of social, economic and political life affects just about everyone. And since labor action is primarily motivated by the wage earners' outlook, it does not, and cannot be expected to coincide completely with the legitimate interests of all other groups and individuals in the nation. Thus the latter inevitably try to influence labor's course.

True, union leaders as a rule resent outsiders "butting in" and tend to denigrate them as meddlers. But the leaders cannot avoid taking cognizance of public opinion and pressures, particularly when they emanate from competent, knowledgeable, and friendly sources. There is, in fact, a mutually rewarding area of contact with the union movement for students, teachers, and other professionals who are generally sympathetic to labor's central aims; it needs increased cultivation.

The general problems in which labor is involved are not its exclusive property, for they include such issues as democracy, social legislation, fair use of power, ethical standards, the public interest in labor-industry relations. In these matters intelligent unionists recognize the value of a give-and-take approach—or should. But a greater effort is needed to bring pro-labor "outsiders" into more intimate intellectual association with the house of labor. The universities and the unions have a world to lose if their present *apartheid* continues. Above all, unionists and non-unionists alike must accept one central, all-conditioning fact, the reality of the ongoing revolution of our time and its speed-up in the final third of the century.

"The world's most important fact is that we are in a revolution," wrote Julian Huxley in his *On Living In A Revolution*. And he pointed out that ". . . we need clear principles, but the resulting system cannot help being an evolutionary one and its detailed working must be constantly supervised and adjusted as it develops." Those words, written twenty-five years ago, are valid today.

Ours, now, is a multiple revolution: war on poverty; abolition of racial inequities; creation and defense of a viable form of democracy rather than of rigid adherence to any particular type of parliamentarianism; coping with the explosion of research, science, and technology; conquest of space; controlling mass population and pollution increase; saving the individual's individuality from the repression of mass-culture, mass-media, mass-living.

Ours is also a crisis of conscience. If, in Franklin D. Roosevelt's era, "the generation had a rendezvous with destiny," each individual today has such a rendezvous. No President of the

United States can serve as proxy for a people. Even a leader who demonstrates, as did Presidents John F. Kennedy and Lyndon B. Johnson, his awareness of the fateful days through which we live, cannot prevail unless each of us, on his own, holds hands with history in the making. As Julian Huxley so aptly suggested: "The remedy is to think in terms of change . . . introduce the time-dimension in our politics and economics, to think in terms of direction and rate of change instead of blueprints or defined systems, however ideal."

It is this pragmatic approach that has ever characterized labor's most forward-moving elements. There still are "miles to go" and a full day's work ahead for the willing and diligent.

LABOR LEADERSHIP IN THE UNIONS
AND IN SOCIETY

The natural habitat of labor leaders is not restricted to the unions that constitute their power base but includes the larger society into which their activities unavoidably extend and of which the unions are a component part. Community participation on the local and national level has indeed become an integral function of labor leadership. The unions have an obvious interest in the successful operation of the enterprises that employ their members and in the socioeconomic health of the communities in which they live and work. Moreover, since collective bargaining and industry-labor relations are ever more strongly conditioned by legislative factors, the unions have accordingly increased their political activities.

There is nothing new about labor's efforts to influence the legislative process, a practice that Felix Frankfurter long ago described as "pre-Victorian." Today labor's pressures on state legislatures and the Congress have simply become stronger, more sustained, and generally more visible, although not always more successful, than in the past.

In one of Frankfurter's notable dissenting opinions, the late Supreme Court Justice noted established precedent for labor's political activities, citing passage of the Adamson Act in 1916 (which established the eight-hour day for the railroad industry) as "positive proof that labor may achieve its desired result through legislation after bargaining techniques fail."

Labor's political proclivities have, of course, been evident ever since the first labor leaders discovered that the same muscles involved in walking a picket line could also propel them to Capitol Hill, and sometimes with more telling effect. Nor was labor slow to discover that in certain situations the muscles needed only to be flexed for the legislators to get the signal.

In 1916, this writer was privileged to witness the political persuasiveness of union power on the Congress of the United States, observing from the gallery the final vote on the Adamson Bill, later cited by Justice Frankfurter. More importantly, the railway union chiefs were present, too. It was no secret that they had previously issued an ultimatum to the effect that if the bill were not passed by 4 P.M. that very day, every rail line in the country would be struck. All details had been arranged; strike-call telegrams were ready to go, pending the outcome of the vote. Now, seated in the gallery, the union leaders silently watched the legislators on the floor below, the clock on the opposite wall, waiting for the speeches to end and the vote to be taken. At precisely 4 o'clock, just as the minute hand reached XII and not one second before, the "Ayes" had it. The performance, for all its drama, was neither the first nor the last demonstration of the pragmatic verity of Frankfurter's opinion that "It is not true in life that political interest is irrelevant to and insulated from economic interests. It is not true for industry or finance. Neither is it true for labor."

Except for enlarged activity, more energetic follow-through, and some refinement in tactics, little has changed in labor's pursuit of political aims since its strong-arm methods forced Congress to establish a shortened work day for the railway industry. But half a century later, the unions have yet to develop a political identity of their own. A labor party is not the answer. A labor program could be if it were broadly inclusive and sufficiently radical (in the sense of going to the roots of society's longtime crisis problems) to challenge the imagination and support of both union members and the most alert, forward-looking elements of the general public. Unfortunately, while the simplistic old "more" non-program is still adhered to in the economic field, despite its obvious inadequacy even there, as exposed by inflation's law of ever-diminishing buying power, in politics "something" is still considered good enough; and this in a period commonly described as "the revolution of our time."

The phrase, of course, has many meanings. And many of those who use it most frequently, not excluding our literary revolutioneers, some social science experts and the Madison Avenue "image" salesmen-cosmeticians, really anticipate a well-mannered upheaval which will nonetheless stand history on its head. (To understand a speaker it is well to observe the way he lives as well as to listen to his words.) But history may be inconsiderate enough to unfold in a more disorderly manner than is currently anticipated, just as it confounded the prognosticators of the 1920s who were forced to eat their own forecasts of violent revolution by the end of the 1930s.

One of the central stabilizing domestic developments of the 1930s and 1940s was organized labor's coming of age, the fact that the union movement grew big and powerful in those two decades. Among many contributing factors, the Magna Carta for organizing in the National Industrial Recovery Act must not be forgotten. But with power came responsibility. Power does not stay put; it is either utilized for large objectives or dissipated in two-by-four gestures. Summing up the state of the unions towards the close of that period, economist Sumner H. Slichter, who was neither a Marxist nor a starry-eyed liberal, said:

> The labor movement which has developed in the United States in the last fifteen years . . . is the largest, the most powerful and the most aggressive that the world has ever seen; and . . . the strongest unions are the most powerful private economic organizations in the country.
>
> (*The New York Times Magazine*, May 16, 1948)

In view of labor's militant temper and rapid expansion in the 1940s, and since four out of five members of the labor force were by then payroll employees constituting a majority of the adult population, Slichter indeed foresaw "a laboristic society in the making." In the article referred to above, he said:

> . . . a community in which employees rather than business

men are the strongest influence . . . will have its own way
of looking at things, its own scale of values, its own ideas
on public policies and, to some extent, its own jurisprudence.

Twenty years later, Slichter's "laboristic society" had failed
to report for duty; nor is there any sign of its doing so in the
foreseeable future. This is not because the concept itself was
unsound but because its realization would require a change in
value judgments which, in turn, would require labor leaders to
take the lead in advancing the thinking of the rank-and-file, This
they were obviously not inclined to do in the get-ahead 1940s,
in the dollar-happy 1950s, nor in the strained and sobering 1960s.
In all three decades, staying put was the unwritten law of the
land. Certainly the employers did not propose to resign from
prosperity and power. Nor were the workers disposed to go out
after an unknown bird in the bush when they thought they had
one safely in hand; in this union policies were not very provident.
        Arrested numerical growth was one effect of the soft 1950s.
For although millions of new workers entered the labor force
each year, soon after the start of the decade membership rolls of
almost all unions became and remained static. Admittedly organizing was becoming more difficult and costly once the first big
crop was in; nor did the Taft-Hartley Act help. But this did not
justify the atrophy of organizing activities in the 1950s; the
unions had ample financial resources for major campaigns. Some
were even confronted by the problem of finding safe, profitable
investments for surplus funds. Very few, however, seemed to remember that their best investments were the big organizing campaigns by which their once-small organizations had become large
and powerful.
        Otherwise, and on the credit side, labor was not entirely
unresponsive to the imperatives of the 1950s. Its leaders responded
both nationally and internally to the Korean "police action." The
uneasy AFL-CIO merger in 1955 was not achieved without prolonged effort and its continued existence is a matter of almost
constant effort, for the alliance, as was obvious from the start,
is anything but a cozy domestic arrangement. And throughout

the decade management did its best to keep labor on the alert. The unions' hold on their members, first tested unsuccessfully by the Taft-Hartley Act, was further and repeatedly challenged by management, most notably in the steel industry; the efforts failed. Union members stood by their unions.

The unions held their own through the 1950s and on through the 1960s. The members remained faithful, and good returns on union dues, including higher pay and fringe benefits, together with increased public acceptance of unionism, further buttressed membership allegiance. But, as experience during these two decades has more than a few times demonstrated, undiscriminating and uninformed union loyalty is a dubious blessing. Unless union members develop genuine understanding of the overall significance of unionism with the ethical implications and obligations thereof, unless they grasp the meaning of union power, its proper purposes and uses, they tend to remain as loyal to corruptly led unions as to those that are not. Jimmy Hoffa's continuing influence on the teamsters, despite his extended sabbatical in jail, derived in no small measure from the failure of the leaders and membership to really understand what unionism is all about. Stated another way, the resultant intellectual poverty is due to the failure of the leadership to cultivate a broad understanding of unionism among the rank-and-file. Intellectual poverty pockets are prevalent throughout the labor movement, scarring even many of the clean and genuinely honest unions. The term "intellectual," as used above, relates to stimulating in the membership an appetite for information about the broad goals and methods of the union world; of developing among the members an awareness of the morality of solidarity as distinct from its heuristic values; of educating the members to an understanding of why "more" is not and never can be the total content of union life, and of promoting membership participation in mental activities geared to goals beyond being a good shop steward. Indeed such intellectual underpinning of unionism might not inconceivably also produce better shop stewards.

The fact is that every union leader worth the title must be a teacher as well as a diplomat, warrior, bargainer, banker, social planner, strategist, and dreamer. In the old days of the Jewish needle trades unions, the leader also was a preacher and the union

hall was a kind of synagogue and center for intellectual dispu-
tation and mutual help. The whole movement could use some of
that spirit today. David Dubinsky, coming out of the old Jewish
Socialist union background, retained many of its qualities. Walter
Reuther, product of a first-generation immigrant German Socialist background, similarly embodied these qualities, as did A.
Philip Randolph, perhaps the most deeply rooted of the three
in the underclass life of American poverty which is mostly ignored by the union movement. There are others, too, who have
genuine leadership qualities, and not all of them are in the over-60
generation.

Individual unions in special trades and situations, and some
unions led by exceptional leaders have escaped the intellectual
deprivations from which the union movement as a whole suffers,
and for which unionism in America has, in a real sense, mort-
gaged its future at insupportably high and also ever-increasing
interest rates. The mental poverty of union life is, of course, not
restricted to it, but permeates and is in fact even greater in
American society as a whole, organized as it is on the basic
fallacy that self-interest is the mainstay of the public good. Although the labor segment in some ways can be said to have lived
significantly in the '50s and '60s, it failed, however, to stretch
its mental muscles as it did in the '30s. True, some academic pundits and union stalwarts decry any effort by labor to "reach for
the stars"; but precisely that kind of stretching exercise is the
categorical imperative of labor dynamism. Unions either advance
or stagnate.

The need for working in the broader social area beyond
the bargaining table raises three central questions. One, has the
union movement the wherewithal to enter the field? Two, toward
which specific areas of national life should labor direct its
efforts? Three, what special aptitudes must the leadership develop
among the rank-and-file to secure active membership participation in the larger democratic society in which the unions function?

The most accurate answers, of course, are in the doing, in
the trial-and-error process by which true knowledge is gained.
But this writer's *ad hoc* hunches, as already indicated, are that
yes, the union movement does have the capacity and indeed, the

necessity to move, no holds barred, into the great tasks of the reconstruction of American society, including its economy, along truly viable democratic lines so that institutions become responsive to the needs of the citizenry and not only to elite and special-interest groups. In so doing, the unions must work with students, liberals, and all underprivileged groups, with minorities such as rural farm workers and the black urban poor, and with majorities such as working women and the "new poor," including senior citizens who have dropped out of the middle class.

If organized labor fails to rally its natural allies to meet this fateful challenge of making democracy work in the onrushing '70s, there is literally no other segment of society to take it up. The students may be willing, but they are powerless (demonstrations, bomb-throwing, and sabotage are not substitutes for constructive action). And lack of power corrupts no less than absolute power. Lack of power is the trough of desperation at which unreason, anarchy, fanaticism, nihilism and other related malignancies of the body politic feed. Students and labor together could become an irresistible force for the transformation of existing political, cultural, and economic institutions into genuine organs of democracy.

Those students who at risk and sacrifice of life helped advance the Civil Rights movement, starting with the Montgomery bus boycotts of 1955 on through the tasks of political and economic education and voter registration during the 1960s, wrote history and in so doing exercised power. Students of the 1970s may well be proud of that legacy as they pick up the urgent tasks of continuing to democratize American society, an assignment in which, as noted earlier, labor is their natural ally.

As to the specific areas of national life toward which labor must direct its efforts, some of these are discussed in this chapter and others of a more complex nature will be examined in later chapters.

*   *   *   *

But now a definition: The term "democratic society" is used throughout this book to denote the nation *in toto*, including all its local and national components, some of which are obviously more "democratic" than others; the essence of a democratic society is, of course, people and has never been more accurately defined than by Abraham Lincoln when he called for "government of the people, by the people, for the people."

That definition, not unnaturally, is often fulfilled by the law of detours. For the course of democratic society, governed though it is by laws subject to revision by prescribed procedures, is yet as complex and not infrequently as contradictory as life itself. Its dynamics are affected by transitory moods, enduring drives, the interplay of new and old lifeways, institutions and philosophies, all of which in turn are subject to the impact of sustained efforts and improvisations by organized groups and of exceptional individuals. Motivations range from the most base to the best, from the most selfish to the completely unselfish. Society is the workplace where the greatest good and worst evil of which people are capable is hammered out. Democratic society lives dangerously and often needs to be saved from itself—by itself.

Labor leadership could usefully assign a task force for the sole purpose of helping society extricate itself from the intellectual swamps into which it occasionally stumbles and in which it is currently lost. The role of such a task force would be to counter the polarization, isolation and rage-apathy syndrome now threatening to destroy us.

America today is, of course, light years away from the America of the 1930s before Franklin D. Roosevelt, with an assist from the labor movement, reshaped and redirected its course. The change was organic, deriving from a modified power structure with new inter-relationships of social groups and forces. The welfare state propensity of American society today had its genesis in the 1930s; despite considerable subsequent expansion, its optimum development is not even in sight. Implicit in the concept of the welfare state is a belief that society has responsibility for sustaining the life and well-being of the individual; but the latter is not, or should not be, merely a recipient of social security payments and benefits. He is also a donor, through his sense of citizenship, to the basic security of the state itself. Mutuality is essential if the distribution of welfare benefits is not to degenerate into a modern version of the old Roman handouts of bread and games. The need for establishing and maintaining a relationship of reciprocal responsibilities between the individual and the state is a crucial area for labor leadership, quite beyond what can be directly achieved within the unions themselves.

Our affluent society is rich beyond compare. Despite great and continuing productivity, it is nowhere near realizing the limits of its capacity. At the start of the century the median annual income of an urban family was 651 dollars; by midcentury it was 4224 dollars after taxes. In 1968 the median urban family income was 9924 dollars in current dollars. From 1947 to 1968 median income for all families (rural and urban) went from 3000 to 8600 dollars; in constant 1968 dollars, median family income went from 4700 to 8600 dollars. Although the purchasing power of the dollar shrank by 34 percent during the first half of the century, the rise in income enabled a family to buy more than double the quantity of goods and services in the 1950s than a comparable family could have bought in 1900. In contrast to the trend in the first half of the century, the rise in earnings and output in the second half has not yet produced any striking increase in the amount of goods and services that the average family can buy. The prospect, as the 1960s drew to a close, was for continued diminution of real wages.

The steady rise in income of the average urban family prior to 1960 was not unearned. According to the U.S. Department of Labor, the individual American worker's output in the forty-hour week in 1960 was "three times that of his grandfather in a 70-hour week span." By the year 2000, the great grandsons can be expected to make an even bigger productivity leap, given the mounting acceleration in automation and the computerization of industry and services.

Much of the earlier stark poverty has been reduced. The average living standard is good; but people do not live by statistical averages. It is no secret that our affluence is inadequately distributed.[1]

The limited spread of American affluence reveals the need for leadership with both the will and capacity to halt the continuing process of economic polarization. Labor is a natural source of such leadership, for union members probably make up a sizable part of that proportion of wage workers who earn from 7000 to 12,000 dollars annually. The security of these workers requires that earnings be increased in the near-poverty and poverty groups. Economic action alone cannot correct the imbalance. This situation, so threatening to the entire citizenry and to organized workers in particular, demands of labor a degree of politicalization and a thoughtful orientation towards the whole of society hitherto only sporadically attempted.

In undertaking this task, labor cannot avoid facing up to a basic change that has developed over the years in our system of government. Without benefit of Constitutional amendments, the political power structure has been reconstituted so that the government is no longer truly representative. According to the Constitution we are governed by an Executive, a Legislature, and a Judiciary. In fact we are also governed by a whole galaxy of regulatory commissions and special task agencies that were created by Congress, and which are in effect endowed with administrative and also quasi-legislative and quasi-judicial authority. Catapulted into public life by the compulsion of evolving economic realities, the Federal Trade Commission and Interstate Commerce Commission, the Securities and Exchange Commission, and many other such institutions add up to a very powerful fourth branch of government.

And there is a fifth adjunct to our supposedly three-way system of checks and balances; it consists of lobbies and pressure groups. Lack of official status in no way diminishes their far-reaching power on the legislative structure of our lives. Hundreds of national organizations maintain lobbies in Washington and in the state capitals. There are far more lobbyists than Congressmen in the nation's capital.

The trade associations, business, professional, farm, labor and other pressure groups, hired the lobbyists that crowd our legislative halls to meet the need for adequate protection of their respective interests. The more powerful of these interests moved into power vacuums created by the inability—or at times the unwillingness—of elected political representatives to fulfill their functional duty of service to their constituents. Each of these lobbies, many expending vast sums of money, seeks to advance its own interests, sometimes acting alone, and sometimes joining with others for specific ends. The process of government tends to reflect the sum of power behind these pressures.

Congress and state legislatures are thus saddled by an extra-legal Third House of blocs and pressure groups that never meets as a body, has no presiding officers, standing committees, nor responsibility to the electorate. Yet these groups are indeed very much part of the nation's governing process. Labor can and should take the lead in seeking to remedy this intolerable state of affairs.

As the world's leading industrial nation, we have a complicated, challenging system of interests, and relations involved in those interests. We still have local or district needs and problems of day-to-day living in a democracy that are met by such institutions as schools, churches, and cultural agencies. But for most Americans the major, vital problem of earning a living ceased to be centered in the community long ago. These economic interests transcend town, county, and state boundaries. Indeed, due to the rapid advance of technology and international interdependence, they are barely contained within the nation. Thus, for example, voters represented by Congressman X— of the district where they reside, more often than not derive their livelihood outside the community, and their major economic interests even may lie outside the county, sometimes outside the state. Furthermore, two chemists, for example, in widely separated cities, as Chicago and San Francisco, may have more in common, so far as their basic economic interest is concerned, than either has with next-door neighbors of differing occupations. Conscientious members of Congress accordingly find it increasingly difficult, and sometimes impossible, to find out just what their constituents want them to do on particular issues. Occasional visits to home territory generally yield contradictory information. And the daily mail of a Senator or Congressman, if he is taken seriously by his constituents, is as diverse as our economic life itself.

When groups of voters call on a member of Congress to secure his support or opposition on a particular legislative measure, they are generally not comprised of neighborhood groups, but of persons from across the country bound by a common interest. It is not geography, but their work, their business, labor or professional concerns, the technology and economics of those concerns, or a common social cause, that brings them together as a unit. A member of Congress cannot tell whether these visitors represent a majority or minority of his own state or district. All he does know is that they have shared economic, cultural, or social interests. Unavoidably, in today's world, a member of Congress must think and act in national rather than in local terms.

Even if all of the long-overdue reforms of Congress, including reform of the seniority and committee systems, were carried out, this central problem would remain.

As presently constituted, members of Congress are unable to come into living touch with the major industry, labor, and other central occupational and professional interests of their constituents. Except for the representatives of a few sparsely settled and underdeveloped areas, a direct, intimate relationship no longer exists. The whole Congress has not enough money to buy the required dynamic competence and knowledge; nor are filing cards and research any substitute for the fresh-breathing data of life. A House of Functional Representatives, made up of delegates from the major industries, the professions, the unions, might enable Congress to be more truly responsive to the nation's needs. Such a steadily evolving "Second House," comprised of representatives from the specialized lines of grass-roots interests and productivity, checked and counter-checked in continuing conference and efforts at adjustment of conflicting outlook, could be established to give the individual legislator information directly concerning the realities of the day, and increase his effectiveness in Congress by enabling him to keep his hand on the heartbeat of the nation's productive life.

A House of Functional Representatives along these or similar lines would not conflict with nor duplicate congressional functions; it would rather complement them. The creation of this Second House also would end the costly game of blocs and lobbies in which labor, like every other national power segment, is presently engaged. The trade-union movement alone cannot halt this practice, but it can spearhead a broadly representative effort to correct the resultant dilution and near-dissolution of the legislative function.

The anticipated opposition of even such vastly wealthy and powerful lobbies as those of the American Medical Association and the National Association of Manufacturers can be overcome, as it has been overcome in every piece of progressive legislation passed by Congress in the last twenty-five years. Democracy can and must be brought up to date by weaving the socially positive functions of the power blocs (whose constant struggle is one of the essentials of democratic government) into a coherent, constitutionally responsible framework of operations.

The organization of a House of Functional Representatives is a major task for a generation. It is collective bargaining with history, calling for education of the citizenry at large and their enlistment in securing the necessary constitutional changes for a tricameral legislature. Short of such action, the invisible legislative powers of the lobbies will continue to fill the present vacuum. This is an area in which labor leadership can be most usefully applied to the benefit not only of labor but of the entire national community.[2]

The pursuit of basic group interests essential to survival in a competitive society should be protected so long as the social fabric is not threatened with destruction and so long as democracy itself and individual rights are preserved. Under the law, all citizens are theoretically equal; but in practice some are obviously more equal than others, at times markedly so. Those who are less equal inevitably struggle against built-in inequities in the law and in life. This applies not only to Negroes, numerous as they are, but also to labor, powerful as it. And there are others who are similarly bypassed. A balance of social forces is of course essential to the democratic process. And since in both economics and politics only equals can bargain effectively, democratic societies tend to be most stable when the correlation of contending forces is most fluid, with ample elbow room for all. In a period of sharp social change like the present, labor certainly cannot afford to be less dynamic than the national scene itself. Actually labor leadership can, if it will, play a central role in strengthening the girders of our democratic, swiftly altering society.

Leadership Within And Beyond The Unions

The union leaders' performance on the home front is to some extent a measure of their impact on the larger society. Perhaps the most accurate, and surely the most authoritative assessment of the relation of labor leaders to the union movement and the world around the unions was made by Walter P. Reuther some years ago. In his opening address to the 1959 convention of the AFL-CIO's Industrial Union Department, Reuther urged the assembled 200 top and next-to-top officers of the seven million members in the IUD-affiliated unions (about half the AFL-CIO membership at the time) to face up to central issues, none of which have since been resolved and all of which have since become even more compelling than they then were.

The crisis to which he referred has not gone away; it is still with us and adds cogency to his words, which are therefore quoted at length.

> Perhaps in this hour of crisis we had better look within ourselves because we cannot . . . escape a major responsibility for the changes which have come about to the adversity of the American labor movement and the American people. . . . We are in trouble because America is in trouble economically . . . politically . . . morally. The source of this basic difficulty is that there has come about in America a gross distortion of our system of values as a free society, and the money changers have taken over the temple of government.

Stressing that labor's fate is intimately linked with the nation's, Reuther said:

> We can make progress in America not as a narrow economic selfish pressure group, but only as we facilitate progress for the whole community. Then we share in that general progress.

*　*　*　*

> We know that we can't solve our problems in a limited vacuum. We can't achieve full employment . . . adequate

educational opportunities . . . security and dignity . . . in a vacuum. We can only do these things as we help America do them for all of the people.

On the subject of moral values, Reuther warned:

Moral values are never compromised in one big compromise. It is a slow process . . . of little corruptions taking on the proportions of a mountain if they go unchallenged. . . . This isn't just happening to labor. We are permitting an erosion of the basic system of values as they relate to all of the people of America.

*   *   *   *

We must show that as our capabilities create greater material wealth, they also are giving that greater wealth meaning and purpose and a sense of direction by equating it with social and moral and human values. That is why what the labor movement does is important; not because we are better people, we are not; but because we come upon this place in human history . . . with a set of moral and social values . . . a sense of dedication to these concepts . . . some tools to work with and weapons with which to struggle. . . . That is why we have got to pick up this fight, because if we fail we not only fail ourselves but we fail the whole of America and America will fail the world.

Scoring labor for not mobilizing its resources to meet the challenge, Reuther said:

The labor movement has gotten prosperous. . . . Prosperity somehow does make people a little bit soft . . . flabby . . . We need to . . . tighten up and regain some of the early spirit so that we can get marching again . . . the corruption thing was used by our enemies, built way out of proportion, because for every crook you can find in the labor movement you can find ten in management. But . . . the very way that we got together the day we accepted the Ethical Practices Code was symbolic of our basic problem . . . That we met in the Roulette Room of the Monte Carlo Hotel in Miami, Florida, to adopt the Ethical Practices Codes is a symbol of what I am talking about.

Reuther's realistic appraisal of leadership shortcomings did not dent his faith in labor:

We have all the resources we need. . . . There is nothing wrong with the rank and file. We are the problem, we who are charged with the responsibilities of leadership. We have failed to provide the program essential to getting the rank and file marching.

*   *   *   *

There is nothing wrong with the American labor movement that a little belt-tightening will not cure. . . . The labor movement is . . . dedicated to human service and only as it keeps that symbol bright will it represent the kind of economic, social and political force which can mobilize the moral power of millions of people in meeting these complex and challenging problems.

It is not news that few of Reuther's peers on the labor olympus shared his view. That did not then or ever deter the auto workers' leader from staking out fresh areas of advance which others first criticized and later followed. Time and again Reuther broke new ground not for the auto workers alone but for all of labor and America. The substance of Reuther's 1959 address has direct bearing on the present and the foreseeable future as an apparently rudderless America moves into the rapids of the century's closing decades.

Labor history consists not only of wage and hour victories and the struggle for a better life, but is punctuated also by stretches of intellectual inertia, defeats, and missed opportunities for innovative action. Continued failure of leadership to respond to the imperatives of the day could threaten the whole fabric of specific labor gains together with the democratic institutions under which they were achieved. After all, 1984 is suddenly not beyond the horizon, but coming up uncomfortably fast. Only octogenarians like this writer can be sure of escaping its onset. Youth and the middle-aged may be less fortunate. To them, and also to every concerned person, it is heartening to consider that even a handful of determined leaders, endowed with genuine mental resilience and goodwill, could measurably enlarge democracy and begin the task of making it work on all levels for all segments of society within the decade of the 1970s. Such efforts would have broad-based support. And they might well prevent that Orwellian nightmare "1984" from becoming the reality for which assorted demogagues of the Right and Left are seeking to condition the nation with what can only be described as obscene relish.

Labor is called upon to take up this long-delayed task at a time when former pro-labor attitudes have been largely dissipated. The general public no longer views the worker with sympathy as the underdog, ill-paid and exploited. And in the universities, for reasons explored in Chapter 1, there is a widely prevalent belief that big labor, like big business, is part of the enemy establishment. To change or modify these attitudes would require more than face lifting by public relations plastic surgeons.

The belt-tightening advocated by Reuther, together with a return to first union principles and a simpler mode of life than that to which most contemporary leaders have accustomed themselves, could be a starting point for needed reformation. Miami's Monte Carlo Hotel was indeed an unsuitable site, as Reuther pointed out, from which to issue labor's Ten Commandments on the conduct of union life; nor are any of the luxury hotels habitually frequented by the men who lead labor exactly appropriate for union lunch conferences and get-togethers.

Time was when it could be argued that it helped boost morale to bring workers struggling for a living wage into a costly hotel for a luncheon conference. That time and the inferiority complex that characterized it are past. But too many labor leaders have adopted the expense account life-style of their corporation counterparts as a perquisite of union office. In so doing they waste union funds, of course, and they increase their alienation from both the rank-and-file and the general community, losing influence in both. There is, also, the dubious "special accounting ethics" of otherwise honest men when it comes to deciding just what constitutes a business expense.

At best, ethical practices are more easily recognized than defined, but anyone with taste buds can tell a good pear from one that's gone rotten. The average worker seems to have no great difficulty in discriminating between what is good and what is bad (that is, ethical or unethical) in his union leader's conduct of union affairs.

In a later chapter we shall explore a few instances of the inherent difficulties confronting members who attempt to correct corrupt or merely somewhat less than fully democratic union practices. One of the hard facts of union life is that, to the average labor leader, the dividing line between ethical and unethical behavior can be very tenuous, at times totally blurred. Such faulty vision is perhaps an occupational disease. At any rate there is the further complicating factor of the possessive pronoun; union presidents tend to identify personal interests with "their" union's interest. Too many have an unfortunate predilection for thinking of the union as private property.

Contemporary philosophers do not provide us with clear guides to the ethical life, but some of the ancients do. Socrates, for example, told us that to care more about truth and justice than for wealth and position was the sign of a good man. Obviously, the element of "what's in it for me" cannot coexist with ethical practices. And conversely, ethical practices involve more than not stealing. Perhaps the ultimate example of ethical practice was Socrates' decision to die rather than to escape or turn against an authority that, though it wronged him, had also nurtured him. In the final trial for his life, Socrates cited his poverty as proof of the fact that he had served as truth's gadfly all his life.

And one hundred years earlier, Confucius told his followers

not to look for small advantages because it "prevents great affairs from being accomplished." A steady focus on "great affairs" may indeed still be the surest guide to maintaining ethical standards. Although few today live by the ancient precepts, to the socially conscious contingent at least, commitment to taking a hand in redirecting the course of history in this nation and throughout the world is what constitutes an ethical practice—and anything else falls short of the mark.

The moral bankruptcy of a business-dominated society, the social impotence of our captains of industry, and the almost endemic thievery of their operations have been well documented in Senate Committee hearings and Department of Justice findings. Within that overall corrupted and corrupting atmosphere, it is not easy for labor or for any other sector of society to remain untainted. The effort, however, must be made.

And every so often there are knotty problems of ethics and economics that even a Socrates or a Confucius could not easily resolve. The old homily, "What is good for society is good for labor," has striking exceptions. Thus it may be good for some segments of society to buy textiles, clothing, radios, baseball bats, refrigerators, cars, and other goods made in Japan and other cheap labor centers abroad, but labor unions in the United States cannot help pulling Uncle Sam's sleeve, and making loud noises in protest. For while it may be good foreign policy to offer a market for the exports of friendly nations, commodity imports produced by cheap labor hit our own labor community in sensitive spots: jobs and earnings. And if, within the United States, some Southern communities, for their own narrowly conceived economic good, choose to grant tax exemptions and build plants virtually gratis, promising cheap, docile workers to a union-tired Northern industry, or pass ordinances against outside troublemakers, meaning union organizers, this is not good for labor or society. That is, we may quarrel with unionists about the specifics of "what's good for labor," but not with its validity as a criterion of labor's approach to management, industry, society. For each social segment of a democracy necessarily promotes its own group interests in the effort to achieve a viable coexistence with the other segments.

So long as the American economy is cramped by "structured"

unemployment, by production purposely operated below capacity, by collusive price-fixing, by rigged bids on government contracts with cost-plus arrangements and the like, so long as built-in obsolescence and the manufacture of pollutants and various disease-and-death-causing products are solemnly included in the Gross National Product, and so long as politicians, including regulatory commissioners, continue to eat out of corporate hands, labor must indeed carefully consider just what is "good for labor" as a condition of survival in a competitive, acquistive world.

Labor leadership's ongoing task is to protect and strengthen labor without damaging the intricate web of democratic society as a whole. As noted earlier, the union leader must not only be a subtle analyst and strategist, but also a teacher of vast, persuasive powers, capable of educating union members and the general public; ethical standards and innovative thinking are basic to the whole enterprise. And, at a time of economic mayhem, the labor leader's overridingly urgent assignment is to reverse the trend of polarization, to close the ever-widening gap between the haves and have-nots which is the Achilles heel of the affluent society, exacerbating every existing point of dissension and divisiveness.

As we enter the final third of the century, millions of blue-collar and white-collar workers are earning more than they ever dreamed of only a decade ago. Yet, as discussed above, they find themselves squeezed by rising prices. They are apprehensive and resentful at the deception life has played on them. To secure their own economic base, this middle-income group must help lift the people who live in poverty and near-poverty closer to their own level. That is, want to or not, the unions must learn, rather swiftly, to identify also with the steadily growing lumpenproletariat or face the possibility of seeing all standards go and their hard-won gains swept out from under them.

In the political arena, labor leaders cannot escape developing basic new orientations to cope with the results of galloping computerization and technology and their effects on old relations. In the decades ahead, only unions not tied by managerial stakes and *status quo* obligations will be able to look history in the eye and make the appropriate adjustments for action in a new world. So far as leadership is concerned, the task is never-ending, but never has the time for action been briefer and more critical than now.

The present situation is not new; its highlights were accurately defined early in the sixties in "Industrialism and World Society": [3]

> Pluralistic industrialism will never reach a final equilibrium. The contest between the forces for uniformity and for diversity will give it life and movement and change. This is a contest which will never reach an ultimate solution. Manager and managed will struggle all up and down the line of hierarchies all around the world; quiet but often desperate little battles will be fought all over the social landscape.

*   *   *   *

> The uniformity that draws on technology and the diversity that draws on individuality; the authority that stems from the managers, and the rebellion, however muted, that stems from the managed—these are destined to be the everlasting threads of the future. They will continue in force when class war, and the contest over private versus public initiative, and the battle between monistic and atomistic ideologies, all have been left behind in the sedimentary layers of history.

Labor leadership has never been a job for pygmies. And responsibility tends to enlarge capacity. Movements, like individuals, earn their way in the action process. Holding hands with the future in the unpredictable closing decades of this century is surely as challenging an assignment as America's union leaders have ever faced.

In seeking to influence the national community, the only authority possessed by labor leaders derives from the intrinsic merit of their concepts and their effectiveness in securing public acceptance and support of these concepts.

Society is not a mailing address, but multitudes of people; thus the realization of any union objective necessarily begins with enlisting the willing, competent cooperation of great numbers of unionists with their leaders on all levels of the union hierarchy. With that first step securely taken, there is a firm base for reaching out into the community.

But the first step is itself a major undertaking, calling for broad education of the membership, and also for a radical overhauling of labor's own communication media and methods. A free labor press is of the essence, and, given the present crisis, is no longer entirely unthinkable. Such a press might not inconceivably even publish reading matter of general interest, in the manner of Edward P. Morgan's free-wheeling news commentaries over radio station ABC between 1955 and 1967 which were subsidized by the AFL-CIO. In view of long-standing traditions, it may not be quite conceivable that the union press and educational performance might be used for purposes other than reiterating the forevertrue views of unassailably virtuous and enlightened leaders. But the times are unprecedented. In many unions a restive rank-and-file are beginning to assert themselves in unaccustomed fashion. There is growing need for an unshackled labor press. Indeed, how can labor ask of society that which it does not consider good enough for itself?

Beyond the confines of the labor world, union participation is already well established in political campaigns and in a variety of philanthropies. But although union members are active in elections and charity drives, many union leaders feel there is only grudging acceptance of their help on the part of the community. A prominent union president expressed a fairly widespread feeling of irritation when he said: ". . . Yes, we raise the money—we give the blood—we build the facilities—we get out the vote. However, having done so we too often tend to withdraw—and in some cases are expected to withdraw—to the background while the bankers, the industrialists, the lawyers and the educators take over as 'members of the board.' And too often we accept it."

Certainly the time has come for labor to be a "member of the board," with a voice in the policy decisions of every organization to which it contributes money and effort.

But there is a built-in obstacle to labor leadership's more effective participation in society. For most of its life, in fact until almost midcentury, labor was forced to live on the other side of the tracks, and accordingly developed an isolation-ward mentality.

Even today, when an occasional labor leader dines at the White House, labor leaders find it difficult to convince union members, and at times themselves too, that active participation in national life, including breaking bread with the President, is indeed consistent with the union's concern for "bread 'n butter." The outworn habit of gearing union goals to the lowest common denominator so that the most backward elements of the membership may not fail to identify with unionism as something really their own and the concomitant concept of shop economics as the journey's end of unionism die hard. But die they must if the American trade-union movement is to come into its majority. It is up to the leadership to set the goals and to adjust the mental vision of the membership to a larger view than now obtains. Far-sighted leaders have more than once taken the rank-and-file with them in their efforts to expand the union world, as the careers of Philip Murray, Walter Reuther, David Dubinsky, Sidney Hillman, and several others eloquently demonstrate.

In the larger community, as in its own realm, unionism now has social obligations that are no less pressing than its economic role. The unprecedented velocity of change continues, it widens in scope, and it cannot be expected to slacken. Never has power been so concentrated and so paralyzed, nor has the gap between wealth and poverty been more evident and more threatening to the institutions of democratic government. Never has so much courage and self-discipline been demanded of a free people, nor has there ever been so much opportunity for diversity and such force for conformity. A tremor of foreboding and also of new possibilities seems to be shaking up the whole of American society as long-accepted values and institutions are questioned and attacked. Against this background, unionism cannot escape its dynamic mission in the larger community. Labor must live with an explosive age. It cannot secede from humanity or escape the choice between growth and dissolution.

INTERNAL UNION DEMOCRACY AND
THE LABOR REFORM ACT

"There are certain primary truths or first principles upon which all subsequent reasons must depend." When these words of Alexander Hamilton's first appeared in *The Federalist* in 1787, they applied to a world whose issues were relatively few and well defined, and in which there was a belief in reason that subsequent events have sharply diminished. But even in an age of unreason such as ours, the use of first principles retains a vestigial cogency. Thus the following discussion of internal union democracy is based on four assumptions or "primary truths." They are:

I. Union democracy is not a *Ding an sich*, a "thing in itself," but a product of the interplay of concepts and forces both within the unions and the national community.

II. As an integral part of the nation in which it functions and by which it is conditioned, the union movement in turn modifies national living patterns in the ongoing effort to secure for labor a more favorable distribution of national power.

III. Unionism in America at age 160, viewed *in toto* and historically, is a progressive, socially motivated force in which job consciousness and "more" are components, but not the alpha and omega of the movement's direction and dynamics.

IV. The problems of internal union democracy reflect the full spectrum of union complexities, not excluding the closely impinging and interrelated issues of leadership, ethics, and labor's pragmatic approach to the aims and means of the entire union enterprise.

The multi-faceted issues of internal union democracy continue to be a nagging and unresolved problem, even though members' rights in their unions have been allegedly protected by federal law for a decade.

Passage of the much-disputed Labor-Management Reporting and Disclosure Act (LMRDA) of 1959 by the 86th Congress has by no means ended the generations-old discussion of whether "there ought to be a law," or whether the union movement could be trusted to police itself and guard the rights of rank-and-file members when violated by unduly power-hungry officers.

The importance of the legislation is undeniable. It makes internal union democracy the law of the land. Two of the Act's seven titles deal specifically with the protection of membership rights. Title I is a Bill of Rights spelling out the rights of union members and sets up procedures for redress in cases of alleged violation. Title IV endeavors to provide for honest elections, limited terms of office, and other generally accepted democratic procedures. The Act's inherent incapacity to fulfill its stated purposes was evident from the start.

Title I posits the right of a union member to enter civil action in a U.S. District Court against his union or a union officer when he believes that there has been a violation or denial of any of his rights under the Act's Bill of Rights for members of labor organizations.

Unfortunately, however, the law fails to provide the means necessary to initiate a lawsuit. Legal action is costly and hazardous, and the individual worker has all odds against him if he dares challenge his union or one of its officers in the courts.

Title IV is more provident. The union member who wishes to complain about an unfair election procedure can file his grievance with the Secretary of Labor who, if he sees a measure of possible validity in the charge, will process the case to a competent court. However, with due and sometimes merited respect for present and future Secretaries of Labor, the Department itself is susceptible to every pollutant in the political air that government agencies breathe. The unions and their officers have expanding power and influence, and while no *prima facie* partiality need be suspected, a misdirected allocation of the benefit of doubt is not impossible. And in view of the natural brotherhood of bureaucrats, the initial reaction to a complainant is, not surprisingly, to view him or her as a congenital troublemaker, calamity howler, or publicity seeker, the standard attitude towards dissenters nearly everywhere.

And it may or may not be mere happenstance that the Act renders lesser aid precisely in those types of infraction where it is most needed. Thus unions whose leadership is generally honest are more likely to tolerate disregard of members' democratic rights than electoral irregularities. Only crooked union officers will tamper with ballots or falsify election returns. The LMRDA, however, offers somewhat more effective protection for democratic elections than for freedom of expression and unorthodox views. But then niceties of the democratic process are not too often given very serious consideration even in otherwise "good" unions. There is the familiar impatience; the union is, above all, a business enterprise, and if a unionist wishes to exercise "fancy, delicate civic virtues," why he can do it elsewhere in the community.

But with all its shortcomings, the 1959 Labor Act is certain to remain in force for years. And since it cannot be expected to have major impact on democratic processes within the unions, the problems of internal union democracy will continue to be a subject of lively concern. It takes more than a statute to solve an important social problem. Moreover, the effectiveness of any law largely depends on its acceptance by the citizens it most affects, on their cooperation and understanding; and on their confidence that its provisions will be fairly enforced. These conditions do not obtain in the case of the LMRDA.

Labor's high command supported early drafts of the law which the then Senators John F. Kennedy and Irving M. Ives guided through the legislative mill. But the unions had no enthusiasm for the final product that emerged with the strong imprint of Senator John L. McClellan's and Representatives Landrum's and Griffin's gift to intra-union democratic safeguards. Labor generally views LMRDA as an uncalled-for and burdensome intrusion by Government in the internal affairs of their free, voluntary associations which, they insist, is what the unions are. To dissenting rank-and-file unionists, as indicated, the law gives an encouraging nod but not a very helping hand.

John F. Kennedy, who presided over the joint conferences

that worked out the final bill "reconciling" conflicting House and Senate versions, said at the time that a much worse labor law would have been enacted had he not consented to irksome changes in his original bill. Kennedy made clear his dissatisfaction by disallowing the use of his name in references to the Act as finally passed.

Available figures of the number of unionists having recourse to the law in the first year after it went into effect, on September 14, 1959, were perhaps a good *ad hoc* measure of the legislation. Under Title IV of the Act, involving democratic union procedures, about 2000 complaints were filed with the Department of Labor, 1700 of them by union members. Only 40 lawsuits were filed in U.S. District Courts under Title I, involving violation of members' rights; only 25 of these cases were fully developed during the year, and in most of them the court declined jurisdiction for a variety of reasons primarily of a technical nature. The "sample" may appear too small to warrant broad generalization. But to this writer it is obvious that the limitations of LMRDA were written into the Act itself, as time and inaction will undoubtedly further demonstrate.[1] Certainly the district courts of the United States have already made abundantly clear their disinclination to encourage this kind of litigation. No welcoming red carpet is unfolded for the aggrieved union member; his road to legal justice is thorny.

Indeed if a union member is to have his day in court, and has no access to non-repayable loans, the wherewithal has to come from an ampler source than his own purse. The law provides that if the plaintiff wins, the court may ultimately require the offender to pay legal costs, including a reasonable fee to plaintiff's counsel. Competent lawyers are not easily retained on such uncertain prospects. Nor can most shop workers meet the other costly expenses of litigation. Conceivably a union-financed defense fund for members' rights could be set up with no tricky strings attached, or a free court service might be established, such as an Office of Public Defender.

But there is another and more significant inadequacy of the courts as presently constituted to adjudicate labor cases under the provisions of Titles I and IV of the LMRDA. Not all complaints of irregularity of elections can be resolved by recounting ballots or by reviewing the observance of relevant procedural prescripts: there are more brutal and also more subtle ways of influencing voters or of sidetracking nominations of opposition candidates than by fraud or open threats; sometimes these more devious methods involve complex human relations rather than violations of law and sometimes they involve terror and the possibility of murder.[2]

Judges at present are hardly equipped to deal with the new type of litigation, and there is no body of adequate laws on which the judiciary can base remedial action in the kinds of cases likely to develop under the LMRDA Bill of Rights for Union Members. Action under rules of evidence would be well nigh impossible in many cases of this category. Nor are most of these internal conflicts in fact justiciable; many are in the province of social therapy. What is missing and much needed are highly specialized courts and a body of laws that could only be developed gradually out of widely diversified experience in the study and settlement of such disputes between members and officers.

It can be said, without stretching comparison too far, that union conflicts actually resemble, in many ways, conflicts within the family. In both, the bases of contention are generally over power or influence. And in both the union and the family, the essential need is to continue to live together, perhaps even more so in the union than in the family. The courts of domestic relations may thus well be a model from which competent governmental authorities, working with equally competent labor men, could start designing a juridical system appropriate for intra-union conflicts. Operating along lines similar to those of domestic relations courts, in close and unbroken proximity to the bases where conflicts develop, and acquiring a realistic understanding of men and issues, such courts would tend to reduce tensions and prevent conflicts in the measure that "officers and men" would develop, respectively, a growing, more precise appreciation of the right uses of officers' authority and power and of the limits of members' rights beyond which democracy borders on anarchy.

Such specialized courts of intra-union relations might, in time, duplicate the experience of the arbitrators or "impartial chairmen" who compose labor-management disputes in a number of industries. Because of the resultant reduction of friction between workers and employers, it can be said that the arbitrators eventually work themselves out of their jobs. At any rate the longer these chairmen or arbitrators function, the less burdensome their functions become as both sides learn the pragmatic limits of their rights and duties. The very existence of ready machinery to adjudicate differences acts as a restraint on mischief and as a deterrent to abuse of power. Just as the impartial chairmen or permanent arbitrators help create a healthier climate in labor-management relations, it is reasonable to assume that thoughtfully developed, well-functioning courts of intra-union relations would similarly diminish areas of conflict, improving atmospheric conditions inside the House of Labor by fortifying democratic processes in the internal life of American unions.

The assumption that intra-union conflicts and power-contests are best composed by an "outside" specialized setup is supported by the documented experience of the Board of Public Review, established by the million-member United Automobile Workers Union to review and resolve internal union conflicts without intervention by union officers. The BPR has been doing unusually well. Only two unions, however, have emulated the UAW example; the American Federation of Teachers and the Association of Western Pulp and Paper Workers. The relatively small Upholsterers International has a similar review board; it was set up a few years prior to the UAW's.

What Union Democracy Is: Scope and Implications

Union democracy operates in two related areas. One involves the individual rights of members within their union, the other concerns members' rights and interests as these are affected by the union, functioning as representative of the members, in negotiations and dealings with employers.

The membership increasingly makes its voice heard effectively (some claim too effectively) on the results of collective bargaining negotiations, and this aspect of what might be called economic democracy is not in serious jeopardy. The same is not true of internal union democracy, which is the subject of this chapter. The following pages are primarily concerned with the state of individual membership rights, and with tracing the limits and potential of democratic processes inside the labor movement proper.

The distinction between the rights of individuals concerning their internal and external interests is thin and often blurred. The two sets of rights differ in that union members have the actual power to assert and defend their rights when immediate material interests are at stake in negotiations with employers. But they do not have quite that power when it comes to defending individual rights within the union itself.

Although every union constitution defines membership rights in the national and local organizations, very few unions have developed effective, built-in defenses of these rights. In the circumstances internal democracy tends to deteriorate. A member who stubbornly insists on rights beyond the defense of his economic interests gets to be viewed as a nuisance or some kind of crank— or left-winger. Such discouragement leads, in unions as elsewhere, to general apathy, a diminution of membership concern with union policies, which in turn lead to bureaucratization of the inherently democratic union edifice.

The unions in most of the industries, trades and services have, by and large, done well by their members over the years since the mid-1930s. Union members, in turn, have amply indicated, in special votes on the union shop and otherwise, that they have not found union "dominance" oppressive, that terms of employment or the union shop have not been imposed without their consent. The frequent laments about involuntary unionism are a self-serving exaggeration, emanating, with rare exceptions, not from the "involuntary" unionists but from involuntarily "unionized" employers and their apologists.

In nearly all the decent unions, and to some extent also even in several unions whose officers used to be on the calling list of the McClellan-headed Senate Rackets Committee, the members have an opportunity to assert their will and accordingly affect the relevant provisions of collective bargaining agreements. Indeed, as early as February, 1961, *Fortune* reported that "a number of labor and management negotiators have been running into difficulty getting their contracts ratified by rank-and-file employees. Recently, for instance, the members of the Switchmen's Union of North America twice rejected a contract with seventeen railroads. . . . and authorized a strike. After a court issued an injunction against a strike, the union negotiators went back and got a better contract, but once again the members rejected it." Further improvement finally brought a settlement. But such performances, according to *Fortune*, create difficulties: "If the rank-and-file votes down a contract endorsed by the union's negotiating committee and then management improves its offer, the union officers are put in a difficult political position." The rank-and-file seem to worry little about that, at least in some of the small unions. Nor do the officers of almost all unions. For when the members turn down a contract to which the officers had consented, the latter are enabled to return to the bargaining table with increased power. They can then blame their demand for better terms on the members' demonstrated obduracy. And when they return with more "bacon," their prestige and standing with the members is enhanced, a result that can hardly be said to put the officers in a "difficult position," as claimed by *Fortune*.

The membership of many unions has, since 1961 when *Fortune* erroneously viewed the development as rather novel, provided innumerable instances of such free-wheeling, and not always very responsible, independence of the leadership in the negotiation of contract terms. The practice, which, at the start of the decade was comparatively rare, became more frequent as the 1960s moved to a close.

The methods by which the members are accorded the opportunity to participate in decision-making are, admittedly, not always overly democratic. Sometimes the procedure resembles the Bolshevik concept and practice of "democratic centralism." But no matter how much the process may, in actual practice, veer towards the autocratic, the members must eventually be more or less satisfied. No leader can avoid coping with this abiding aspect of democracy; for if the men in the work places are displeased, they can slow down on the job, curtailing the officers' ability to "deliver" under their contractual commitments to management.

Members participate in decision-making in these essentially economic matters through discussions at local union meetings.

Even more participate, usually, at special in-plant meetings held after work hours. The union officers present their proposals for approval by the in-plant meetings, allowing time for questions and for dissenting views. The possibility that members may vote down the proposals tends to restrain high-handed bureaucratic assertiveness. The making of general union-management contracts, when the members have their say, is only the first stage in collective bargaining, and generally takes place every two or three years. The second stage in collective bargaining is the application of the general terms of the contract to particular situations and circumstances, as they develop in day-to-day shop relationships. Although a vital part of the bargaining process, this is less conspicuous, for it no longer involves the entire working group covered by the contract. The latter no longer takes part in decision-making, action being now restricted to "the organization," that is to the officers, from local business agent down to shop steward or shop committee. Much power is exercised in this phase, and a member not favored by those in authority can be given enough squeeze to make continuance of "wrong," "misguided," or simply irritating behavior, difficult, even to the point of jeopardizing his job. However, even in these instances the unionist is not altogether without a measure of protection. The shop stewards or shop committees are "of the people and by the people" and are generally readily disposed to act "for the people." They are members of the shop society, an informal constellation of power, which careful-thinking union officers do not casually antagonize.

A union member's economic interest obviously can be defined with relative ease as compared to most of his democratic rights within the union. To facilitate effective protection, these latter rights require clear definition and thoughtful consideration in their immediate relation to the function and procedures of the group. This is no easy task, nor can it be done once and for all in the forever evolving circumstances of American life. The bill of rights in Title I of the LMRDA offers a good enough definition of the essentials of internal union democracy, but as indicated, it fails to provide workable means for their protection.

Stated in general terms, the scope of internal union democracy by and large comprises the following rights of the union member:

1. to participate through chosen representatives in the government of his union;
2. to stand for, and hold union office on such conditions and within such qualifications as determined by the union's own rules, democratically enacted;
3. to vote on the basis of uniform rules in local and national elections and on all decisions by local and national bodies which are subject to vote by the members under the union's constitution;
4. to express individual views on all matters before the union for consideration and on such which a member deems to be consistent with the union's interest and consequently worthy of consideration;
5. to advocate change of policies and personnel in the union's government.

Implicit in the exercise of these rights is, of course, the duty of union members to defend their union and comply with its governing rules.

It is not a thesis of this review that the union movement is generally deficient in democratic practice. Perhaps internal union democracy is not weaker, across the board, than is the democratic process in other segments of the national community, those which are generally referred to as voluntary associations. Quite likely labor has even a better record on this score. But actually it is not possible, in good logic, to consider the unions simply as private voluntary associations, such as the National Association of Manufacturers, the American Medical Association, the American Legion, or the American Bar Association, although they, too, like the unions, seek to protect and advance their members' interests.

The adjective *voluntary* is no longer quite applicable to unions in view of legislation enacted in the last three decades. These laws protect the workers' right to organize; obligate employers to bargain in good faith with a union chosen by their employees; recognize that there is a widening scope of issues that can be bargained over, some of which were formerly considered management's exclusive prerogatives; and maintain the right of the union recognized by the majority of employees to be the exclusive bargaining agent for all the employees in the workplace, which in effect considerably eases the union's job of inducing even the reluctant to "join up." All this invests the unions with a measure of public power that private voluntary associations lack. Labor's enhanced position under the law of the land imposes upon the unions certain democratic responsibilities: their internal life becomes, to a degree, a matter of public concern. /

The unions constitute, collectively, a major social force which has significantly altered social power relationships in American society. This cannot be said with equal weight about other voluntary, strictly private associations. There is, indeed, a vital qualitative difference, to cite one instance, between the unremitting efforts of the AMA to increase the physician's intake and its persistence in blocking the development of low-cost cooperative health-protection plans on the one hand, and on the other hand the unions' quest for higher wages, for a reasonably limited workday, for health protection, retirement pension, and, what counts most, the unions' contribution to the introduction of order, reason, and plan in labor-management relations, industry and business. The medics' greedy assaults on their patients' dollars have not added nor sought to add to the nation's values' reservoir, whereas organized labor's war on low wages, work hazards, unfreedom and undignity in the workplaces has tended to vitalize the national economy, bringing its political and legislative practices a little closer to the changing realities of American life. /

Of course not all union members, nor for that matter not even all labor leaders, are aware of the broad ultimates implicit in their efforts. It is not unusual for actors in a social drama to be unaware of the implications of the roles they perform. They see themselves, first and last. Unionists are no different from others in this as in most any other respect. That they may not be conscious of making history while laying foundations of office buildings, laundering shirts, or servicing store customers, does not minimize the over-all significance of their efforts. Nor does it lessen the rightful concern of the informed public and the nation's government to know what goes on in the inner recesses of the organizations of the over twenty-million men and women who comprise the union movement, and who are in fact quite a large part of the total adult working population.

Implicit in the concept of internal union democracy is active participation by union members in the union performance, even as the active participation of labor in the nation's development is a constituent of labor's general commitment to democracy. On the whole and over the years, labor has made good on the latter obligation, keeping pace rather better than other sectors of the nation with the changing character of democracy. As the labor movement acquired greater content and momentum, the unions' political orientation expanded. Having at first confined themselves to "political demands," to ameliorative proposals closely bearing on "shop" life, the unions have gradually included in their political programs not a few rather bold ideas bearing on the governmental process, the over-all course of the nation, and on the interrelations of the social components within the nation.

The movement has not performed equally well within its own realm: democracy was short-changed in some unions; dishonesty found a haven in others. The reference is not to unions which fell under Communist party domination and were politically abused, nor to those where racketeers and downright crooks took over. Abuse for political or economic gain is endemic in our society and is not an exclusively union aberration. This does not lessen a legitimate concern when wrongdoings are tolerated in unions whose leadership is genuinely and generally honest.

Democratic rights of members are at times ignored because of institutional considerations or in the interests of so-called efficiency, when it may appear more practical to bypass the time-consuming and often uncertain democratic processes. Also, a personally honest leader, motivated by institutional predilections or fear that open confrontation might endanger the leadership setup or disrupt a going industrial relationship, may sometimes tolerate a part-time corruption, if it is not too conspicuous. He might side-step it, uneasily hoping for someone else to catch the culprit or for the wrongdoer, if not a hardened criminal, to mend his ways.

The concept of "permissible limits of corruption" was originated by once-upon-a-time empire-builders to keep their colonial administrators content and loyal. The concept found its way into the recesses of union government, but it is not a practice that sits well with the larger meaning of unionism. It may ease a leader's stay in power, but it undermines the base of that power by demoralizing the members. Any degradation of the democratic dogma similarly tends to demoralize or to devitalize the union members.

The democratic way of life is not easily operated in "the more perfect union," still less so in the labor union, that state without a land which can be held together and afloat solely by its own moral cohesion. The problem of union democracy thus poses numerous questions, such as:

1. Can the rank-and-file be depended upon to maintain, by its own momentum, a democratic government of unions and to resist usurpation of power by leaders who are either power-hungry, over-zealous, or overly "efficient," or who use union power for private, personal ends?

2. How well equipped are the unions structurally and through their governing laws and procedural practices, as these are affected by federal and state labor legislation, to deal effectively with issues of ethics and democracy in the evolving new circumstances of union activity and outlook?

3. How compatible are democracy and efficiency in the actual operation of union government, and is it at all possible for "big" unionism to function democratically in dealing with "big" industry and expanding "big" government?

4. Can union leadership, at the top level or in the intermediate categories, be relied upon to assure democratic functioning of unions in the face of either total apathy or of only limited members' participation in union affairs?

5. Should not, perhaps, the abstractions of democracy and ethics in the union codes be implemented by developing a kind of "floor" under and "ceiling" over the power of union leaders to protect members, and leaders as well, against wrongdoing by either to the other, or against acts by either inconsistent with union interests?

Certainly all indications are that unionism needs some "basic research" linked with a will to win the battle for democracy in the minds of men in unions as elsewhere. Outstanding labor men, many in commanding positions, have been proceeding from this premise. But it is not evident that much progress has been made towards such a revaluation of values, which may hurt. The House of Labor, like all institutions, rarely has enough objective insight into its own failings. Labor is strong, but not strong enough to be less than fully mobilized on all levels of its pyramidal structure. The sounds of approaching storms grow louder as we approach a watershed in American social and economic history; he wins in the end who heeds warnings first.

Living in a Glass House

Under strong public pressure reenforced by legislation, labor's inner life is now open to public scrutiny. How well are the unions ready to face it?

No valid statistical or factual material is available to assess accurately the state of the internal life of this multimillion segment of our body politic. Nor can it be expected that enough research data will be assembled in our time to indicate with any degree of precision just how many unions there are in which the democratic process is in good working order, or functions poorly, or is altogether in disarray. Sample studies made here and there provide useful material for speculation, but the yield of such studies is insufficient to justify more than *ad hoc* judgments about the democratic actuality in the union movement.

There are probably not many comparable areas of socio-political exploration, if any, where generalizations based on a sample are likely to be more misleading. The union movement's varied multimillions of members belong to over 70,000 local organizations. The members also function in many thousands of delegated set-ups within each of 150 national unions and in a multitude of inter-union councils or federations. Study is further complicated by the diversity of operational ways and methods of this numerically vast assortment of organized labor units.

Moreover it is most difficult, indeed really impossible, to formulate a standard yardstick for evaluating the democratic performance in unions. For what may well be rated as "good" democratic procedure in a small-town local union of a hundred or so craftsmen may prove unsatisfactory or entirely unworkable in a 30,000-member local union of unskilled or semi-skilled unionists in Chicago or New York. And democratic procedures that work well for big-city unions may be disastrous or inapplicable to a mixed union of skilled, semiskilled and unskilled workers em-

ployed in a big plant outside a big city, whose members live anywhere within a 25-mile radius of the workplace and find it a
problem to attend after-dinner meetings of their local.

Responsible labor leaders are not too well pleased with the
present state of union democracy, but they would consider it a
breach of loyalty to make public statements about union shortcomings in this or any other area. The preamble to Code No. 6 of
the AFL-CIO Codes of Ethical Practices, enacted by the Second
Constitutional Convention in 1957, went so far as to say in part:

> The record of union democracy, like the record of our
> nation's democracy, is not perfect. A few unions do
> not adequately, in their constitutions, provide for these
> basic elements of democratic practice. A few unions do
> not practice or implement the principles set forth in their
> constitutions. Finally, while the overwhelming majority of
> American unions both preach and practice the principles
> of democracy, in all too many instances the membership
> by apathy and indifference have forfeited their rights of
> union citizenship.

The statement blamed membership "apathy and indifference"
for the failure of democracy "in all too many instances." No
democracy, of course, can survive the indifference of its constituents. But often enough "apathy and indifference" are engendered
by frustration with machine rule and bureaucracy. Active interest
of the members in union affairs, like citizen concern with democracy in the political state, needs to be cultivated. Left to thrive
solely on a diet of "what's in it for me," participation is quite
likely to degenerate into mean trading deals for "more," with
the junior partners usually short-changed and democracy even
more so.

While deploring instances of membership laxity, the AFL-
CIO bravely affirmed that "the overwhelming majority of American unions both preach and practice democracy." But some
doubts about that "overwhelming majority" must have subsequently developed as the gap between words and deeds became

glaringly and unavoidably evident even to labor's high command. Otherwise its Ethics Committee would not have been given the right to initiate explorations of noncompliance with the code's prescripts and the AFL-CIO would not have been given authority to intervene with affiliates to secure proper performance. The international unions do not willingly or readily yield their exclusive autonomous rights.

Admittedly, "democracy" is an elastic term, changing with time and place. And indeed, the AFL-CIO concept, as expressed in its ethics code, appears to assume that virtually all requirements for internal union democracy would be fulfilled if only all members would regularly attend local union meetings; if officers would call union conventions at the proper intervals as provided for in the respective union constitutions; and also, of course, if the members would always vote at these conventions, or in whichever other ways are specified in their bylaws, for the right kind of officers. The same views prevailed in the long public discussions which preceded enactment of the LMRDA.

There is virtue, obviously, in these props of union democracy, but like all other safeguards of democratic practice, they are not altogether foolproof. Rank-and-file democracy is not self-propelling. "Big unionism" challenges the old defense mechanisms. The individual member, unless he is unusually capable and persistent, does not stand much of a chance to assert his views in local unions that number their members in the thousands and at times in the tens of thousands and are in effect big mass meetings. In these circumstances union government tends to be operated by a small number of members who serve on committees or are otherwise "active," with the bulk of the membership asserting themselves in voting on ready-made motions.

Survival of the democratic process in the rapidly growing "big" unions of our time depends on one of two very infrequently encountered factors: a competent, democratic-minded, dedicated leadership; or a determinedly democratic membership, tough and capable of doing a good day's fighting for a clear issue. Unions are not debating societies; they are out for tangible results. But as members pursue their immediate interests, many unavoidably come to realize how much these are shaped by relevant national forces and issues. With that realization comes a social awareness which differentiates them from the "slot-machine" unionist who puts his dues into the union box buying "a chance" to win a return on the gamble. The committed unionist helps build an organization for economic and social power for the group, of which he feels himself an organic part. This happens where there is cooperation between leaders and members, and where dissent is viewed as a necessary ingredient of consensus.

But happy combinations of members and leaders so endowed with desire and talent for constructive cooperation are rare and require cultivation. Leaders' democratic impulses tend to wear thin under the pressures for speedy, efficient operation. Nor can the democratic proclivities of most members withstand prolonged periods of discouragement and disuse, especially when the leader appears to be "delivering the goods" anyhow.

An extreme case is the performance of John L. Lewis, the mineworkers' leader for four decades. He spoke with characteristic clarity when he argued in the 1944 UMWA convention for continuing the policy of appointing provisional officers rather than electing the presidents of 23 of the 30 districts of the union. The policy had by that time been in force for almost two decades, and it has not since changed.

"I am sick and tired," Mr. Lewis told the convention, "of some of these elected officers in some of these districts, when we ask them why they don't do this or that, and have them tell me 'Why, I am autonomous.' What the hell do I care whether they are autonomous or not? I want action, I want service, I want loyalty."

In 1952 Lewis again defended provisionalism, this time by drawing a parallel between the miners' union and the United States government: "We have in our Republic election of certain representatives by the people, but they don't elect the 2,000,000 Federal office holders in government establishments, because they wouldn't have anything to do but conduct elections and nothing would be settled." By thus equating the union convention with the U.S. Congress, he may have flattered some delegates. But others surely were not unaware that democracy is protected in the United States by separation of powers, a system of checks and balances, the Bill of Rights, and a free press, all of which are virtually nonexistent in union government. However, the majority supported Lewis; he was their leader. And he was not shy to use their support as further argument: "Why, if the majority of the convention delegates and the members back of the delegates dislike provisionalism, they can vote it down, but they haven't."

Again in 1961, a retired but not retiring Lewis told the miners' convention that election of district officers is "an exercise in foolishness." Never an admirer of the niceties of internal union democracy, the miners' chief merely vocalized a widespread attitude of top echelon leadership.

The same attitude informed the testimony before a Senate Labor Subcommittee of the late George M. Harrison, for years President of the Brotherhood of Railway Clerks and one of the most influential leaders of the AFL-CIO. Harrison left no room for ambiguity when he told the Senators:

Local unions, or subordinate local lodges, are in reality simply branches of the international union and subject to its governing laws and supervision. *They do not exist separate and independent from the parent international organization,* but are created by, and are made subject to it through the issuance of a charter. They have only limited autonomy to handle local affairs. In 1935, when the National Labor Relations Act was under consideration, complaint was voiced that international unions and their leaders were failing in their duty to exercise sufficient responsibility and control over their local unions.

*   *   *

Now the hue and cry seems to be in the opposite direction. But it is a dangerous direction because any legislation which, under the name of democracy, encourages local independence from effective control by the parent union unwittingly opens the door of a union to communist infiltration and subversion or irresponsibility. In short, if we are expected to discharge our responsibilities as officials of international unions, *do not deprive us of the means and controls* to do the job.

Obviously, union democracy is not wholly made at the base of the union power edifice, but the unmaking of it begins just there.

Beyond doubt, the great mass of unions both "preach and practice democracy" in the local units. And local activity is indeed extensive; as reported in the labor press, thousands of truly exciting local meetings are held week after week and numerous constructive projects are undertaken, many of them beyond the routine of shop detail. If activity could be identified with democracy, critics would have to seek greener pastures. Unfortunately this is not so. True, the sideline activities of local unions can be useful training exercises for the members as unionists, but unless such activities bear on power relations within the union, they are, of course, no index of the functioning—or malfunctioning—of internal democracy. And if they divert membership attention from union affairs, the union's democratic health is inevitably impaired.

Local union democracy is not spontaneously generated and indeed requires careful cultivation. Most workers obviously join unions for economic advantages, and not because of a general interest in democracy or its functional techniques. The worker first of all wants freedom from the employer's unconditional power. But his appetite grows with the eating. He soon reaches out for citizenship in the work place and for status within the limited meaning of the term as applied to the shop. He looks for means to survive as an individual despite the leveling and depersonalizing effects of the modern industrial plant.

As the contents of unionist expectancies expand with national economic and technological growth and with increased union power in what is sometimes overenthusiastically referred to as the "welfare state," the union member, like all so-called economic men, becomes ever more political. Of course, job and work terms continue to be his first interest. But he comes to realize, at first vaguely, and then with increasing clarity, that government economic, fiscal, and domestic policies, and foreign policies and issues too, are intimately involved with the size of his pay check and what it can purchase. Of recent years there has also been a painful, increasing awareness of the effect of foreign manufactures and policies on American industry and industry-labor relations.

This widening focus produces a "whole man," a citizen-worker-unionist. The member no longer sees himself nor is viewed by others as three separate entities: so many hours a "working stiff," so many hours a family man, and the few remaining hours a citizen who is part of the working community. He begins to see himself as all these things all the time. The union officer similarly no longer views himself as merely a "pork-chopper." He becomes a public personality, complex and socially aware. The union itself becomes involved in a widening scope of broad concern and activity. Even purely moral stances sometimes emerge as by-products of a by now rather sophisticated outlook. The refusal of the longshoremen to handle cargo or baggage of Soviet ships and ships of Communist-controlled countries was in the nature of a moral boycott yielding no private advantage.

Against this background, the "limited" or pure-and-simple unionism, long considered by some intellectual pundits as tailored just right for Tom, Dick, and Harry, has begun to expand—or, shall we say, disappear? On the other hand, how can a hypothetical entity which never had a counterpart in the reality of union life be said to cease to exist? For the fact is that the Gompers-Commons-Perlman axis on which the union world was said (and by some is still said) to revolve a half century ago was then, as it is now, a figment of stubborn imagination.

In any case, the once-proletarian trio are now Messrs. Tom, Dick, and Harry. Having developed political curiosity and social taste, they now wish to serve on boards of all kinds, even to run for public office. They strive to represent the union, and they are no longer pleased with a pat on the back by lower-rank union officials or by supervisory company men. They want to do a bit of their own "politicking" in the union and on the outside, for whatever this may be worth in material advantage, self-esteem, and increased social status. Not all unionists, but enough to count and matter, have taken on this "new" complexion and character.

These changes account for much of the current precarious state of internal union democracy. A particularly complicating component is the growing intensity of power contests within many unions and among ever so many national unions against each other. Always a congeries of power relationships within and outside, the union movement has become a more intensely power-oriented entity in the age of big business, big government, big labor, big United States. Power disputes and essential policy contests spill over the hitherto seemingly impregnable Maginot Line of national autonomies and jurisdictional defenses.

Unionism is having its own "managerial revolution." Not unlike business, the unions appear to be undergoing a growing separation of management from ownership, of union officerhood from union membership. As the trend mounts, and it does in large areas, a schizophrenic condition has developed in many leaders' minds. They become uncertain as to whether they are agents of a movement committed to social engineering or whether they are merely highly placed merchandisers of a commodity called labor. In the former case the job is to lead, and democracy is part of leadership. But democracy is irrelevant, and in fact a handicap, if the job is solely to sell labor on the best terms obtainable. In the latter case there is that inevitable lessening of membership interest and resultant apathy to which the AFL-CIO ethics code, as quoted earlier, ascribed much of the decline of union democracy.

The quality of democracy prevailing within any union at any given time derives from a mix of leadership habits, attitudes and goals, and membership backgrounds, behavioral habits, and ways of thinking, as these affect the kind of "machine" that the leadership wants to maintain. Obviously, union democracy does not escape the frustrations of democracy generally. But the specific difficulties that beset the democratic process in the labor movement mirror the movement's failure, thus far, to equate its intellectual content and commitments with its enhanced status and augmented power in the nation. Within the 1970s, the movement must at long last catch up with its own growth and the imperatives of that growth for a reexamination of long-established union ways and an adjustment of procedures, policies, and perspectives to altered realities.

Living in a glass house, as labor now does, may give it the advantage of being able to see the outside world. But it also means being seen by it; and no public relations makeup can cover internal deficiencies. Unionism cannot afford to be seen at less than its best at home as well as when it goes out.

4

SOME PRAGMATIC PROBLEMS OF UNION DEMOCRACY

The right to propose changes in the law and of governing personnel is, of course, essential to the democratic process; so too is the art of listening. Every advocate of democracy must, moreover, stand ready to be scrutinized and criticized, even as he himself is prepared to scrutinize and criticize others. This means that dissent must be accepted and dissenters viewed as opponents, not enemies. But since unions, unfortunately, are at best never secure from outside attack, open or veiled, at any time, only an opposition loyal to the union as a going concern is thinkable or acceptable. This modification of a democratic principle is dictated by the reality relation of the unions and society. It imposes difficult restraints on both opponents and supporters of the union administration, as well as on the officers who comprise it.

The opposition must guard against indulging in action that may result in throwing the baby out with the bath water and against shooting from the hip just to keep in practice. The opposition in a union and in a political state are radically different. The business of the political opposition party is to oppose the party in power, and it is often argued that the public interest is thus served; but most of the time only the opposition is served by being kept demonstrably alive. No union can afford this kind of political gaming. The measure of the legitimacy of an opposition in a union is the extent to which there is a vital interest at stake, a matter of principle or personality clearly basic to the union interest. The union administration, in turn, must act against critics and opponents only when there is a real danger that they will do more damage than good and avoid manufacturing bogus enemies only to whip up a patriotic frenzy; its proper function is to listen and to defend only that which, in the union interest, must be defended.

Another requirement for democracy to function fully in the unions is a competent, objective judicial process to resolve conflicts that reach a stage beyond composition by practical compromise. It would seem self-evident that the contending parties cannot themselves, or through their agents, render a just and binding decision. An impartial judgment acceptable to the combatants on both sides can come only from an outside source. Thus the president of a union would seem to be the least appropriate person to act as a court of last resort in a conflict between members of the union and business agents or other representatives whom he himself has appointed and who act on his orders. Within the union movement, however, the thought seems to prevail that any trusted member, if honest and intelligent, can reliably perform virtually any function—judge, prosecutor, administrator, legislator, or several simultaneously.

This belief, or myopia, is characteristic of the union world and was cogently stated some years back in a public discussion of the UAW Public Review Board by the widely respected A. J. Hayes, president of the International Association of Machinists for years and chairman of the AFL-CIO Ethics Committee. Although Mr. Hayes stressed that he spoke only for himself and the IAM, the view he expressed was and still is, with some very rare and notable exceptions, that of labor's high command. It is shared by most of the rank-and-file too. What Mr. Hayes said in effect was:

> A disposition of disputes and contests of members and officers is my responsibility under the union constitution, and I will not "pass the buck" to anybody else.

Not unduly power hungry and a man of integrity and intelligence, Mr. Hayes yet could not see why, although he was the union's chief executive, he should not also act as chief justice in a power contest involving his administration. Hayes considered this a duty and a prerogative of office. But he most certainly would have objected, on the grounds of its being antidemocratic, to any similar commingling of the functions of executive, legislator, or judge in the government of the United States. To Hayes, as to many others, the union had a different democratic logic.

Walter P. Reuther and his colleagues and Sal B. Hoffman of the Upholsterers International Union and his associates, as noted earlier, long ago accepted the view that an interested party should not sit in binding judgment—in person or through a subordinate officer—on an internal union dispute. David Dubinsky, as president of the International Ladies Garment Workers Union, more than once expressed the same attitude when he insisted that internal union disputes be adjudicated by an outside, disinterested agency.

But with these and a few more exceptions, the sentiment against outside "interference" generally prevails, even among men who are no primitives and are in all other respects rather distinguished progressives.

Is this just a blind spot in union thinking, an unaccountable survival of a past long gone? Or is this one more manifestation of the unionists' continuing distrust of the outside intellectual, the egghead who may be employed, paid, and even honored for good services rendered, but who must be kept distant from the inner "family of labor"? An element of retributive justice is not to be excluded. The egghead had indeed sinned. He too often seemed to be affected by some sort of astigmatism when looking at labor and theorizing about it.

Has Labor "Arrived" or Is It Declining?

There was considerable speculation among intellectuals and labor experts in the 1950s and 1960s on the subject of whether the unions had "arrived" or declined. The unions themselves were too busily engaged in keeping alive to contribute much to the debate.

Dr. Clark Kerr, whose outstanding reputation as an educator and labor economist is well merited, was president of the University of California when his twenty-page pamphlet, *Unions and Leaders of Their Own Choosing*, was published by the Ford Foundation Trade Union Project in 1957. With its publication Dr. Kerr appeared to join exponents of the fallacious theory that labor had attained its maximal permissible limits of growth.

Clearly motivated by a concern with restoring to union members some of the freedoms they have allegedly lost under the new mass unionism, Kerr's thesis is based on the premise that unions are now firmly established and generally accepted and that, as he put it, "there are no really dramatic internal crusades today either existing or needed."

But, Kerr stressed, "there are reforms which are both needed and in the making."

According to Kerr, the old fighting "cause" born out of struggling with antiunion employers and inimical government attitudes no longer exists. To substitute for it, and to generally raise the quality of union life, Dr. Kerr proposed a new "faith," one consonant with what he viewed as the enhanced state of the unions.

As a possible source for developing a needed new credo, Kerr proposed:

> Might not the unions turn their attention from the old slogans and the old dogmas, and undertake a new orientation toward their role in industrial society? The new role might well be that of a liberating force in industrial society, of a force helping to build a type of industrialization which would meet the desires of the single individual as well as of the organized group. This would be a mission the employers might well join, for they too have pressed for conformity and against individuality among the workers.

This mission, said Dr. Kerr, "might carry the union leader more into the intellectual and less into the business community."

Many harassed labor leaders would undoubtedly prefer to deal with the Center for the Study of Democratic Institutions

than with the General Electric Company and other giant corporations. But wishful thinking aside, the old slogans and the old
faith still face a long difficult run.

There are two central proposals in the Kerr program to
compensate union members for their release from current and
growing restrictions on their decision-making role due to expanding union powers.

One proposal urges the unions to confine their interests and
activities solely to what concerns the unionists as workers and not
as citizens or as consumers. This limited unionism endorsed by
Kerr would enable union members to make their own choices
and decisions in social areas where the union administrations now
wield most of the authority, thereby, according to Kerr, limiting
the members' freedom.

Dr. Kerr's second proposal for union reform is tantamount to
legitimizing a permanent oppositionary faction. He notes with
approval the practice of the International Typographical Union
in having a permanent opposition party which is recognized and
given equal status with the party in power as regards election
campaigns, space in the union publication, and the like.

Dr. Kerr observes:

> The two-party system within unions is an historical oddity.
> The regularly contested election is a rarity. Yet union
> officials do get changed other than as a result of death or
> retirement. Union officials are, in effect, "hired" by the
> membership for the duration of their good behavior as
> tested imprecisely by the membership.

But, as even Dr. Kerr fully acknowledges, trouble begins
when union officers do not want to be fired. Like the professors
they want tenure and want it even more desperately. An ex-union
president has nowhere to go. Undaunted, Dr. Kerr recommends
ways for coping with this admittedly difficult situation:

1) It must be possible for a faction to form and for its

members to be reasonably free from retaliation through the operation of an impartial judicial process; and 2) there must be secret elections at appropriate intervals. Other actors must be allowed to stand in the wings and be permitted to move on stage when the audience calls on them. The dissatisfied individual and the antagonistic faction must be given an opportunity.

Not surprisingly, Dr. Kerr's ideas promptly drew fire from the labor Olympus. Formally, it was A. J. Hayes who responded as president of the IAM. But, as in the instance cited earlier, there was no doubt that he spoke for labor's high command. The encounter took the unusual form of a review of a university president's pamphlet by a union president in the AFL-CIO bulletin, *Education*, in April, 1958. The Hayes review was followed by Dr. Kerr's comments on it in the July-August issue of the same publication, accompanied by a rebuttal from Mr. Hayes.

Dr. Kerr's prestige among labor leaders accounted in large part for the attention his proposals received. And A. J. Hayes, as chairman of the AFL-CIO Ethical Practices Committee, which deals with problems of internal union democracy, was the obvious person to express the official response. That response, in turn, was much colored by labor sensitivity at the time to public opinion. However, this sensitivity did not deter Hayes from reading the riot act to Kerr and other intellectuals who, the union president said, no longer loved labor as they had in the past, because it was no longer a pitiful underdog but an independent, significant factor in American life.

Hayes did not even consider the Kerr proposal for a permanently functioning opposition within the union and also made it clear that labor would not tolerate outsiders coming in to adjudicate or pass judgment on internal union disputes. He said:

In . . . these days when the labor movement is under such strong and concerted attack, it is difficult for those who seek a middle ground to avoid entanglement with one side or the other.

The argument was a *non sequitur*, since an internal union conflict over authority or rights is in no way relevant to external "attacks on the labor movement." Mr. Hayes, moreover, had been cooperating and "co-existing" constructively with variously shaped eggheads in ventures of significance to the public and to his union for some time; nonetheless he rejected any possibility of outside intellectuals acting independently within the unions.

But Dr. Kerr's proposal for "an impartial judicial process" to help correct some of the malfunctions of internal union democracy could not be passed over lightly. In this area Kerr was eminent as a thinker and doer, having been a key architect of the UAW's Board of Public Review before serving with distinction on it. He had first-hand knowledge of the paradoxes of internal union democracy. And when it came to the practical problems of protecting the democratic rights of union members, his credentials were impeccable. Nonetheless, Dr. Kerr was still something of an "outsider"; he came from the academic world.

Hayes did not flinch from taking serious issue with the view that the union situation was completely stabilized, which was the basic premise of the Kerr proposals.

Rejecting the notion that labor had "arrived" and should therefore wear an ideological strait jacket, confining its activities solely to union and management relations, Hays wrote:

> In Mr. Kerr's mind, obviously, there is no such consideration as the 27-million unorganized workers in the country, or the "right to work" movement, or the concurrent campaign to muzzle labor politically. Or, if these things do exist, they are of no importance to him . . .
>
> Men are men, however they may be split into component parts by academicians, and the working men and women of America will continue in the future, as they have done in the past, to use their unions as their effective spokesmen in whatever sphere of life—economic, social, cultural, legislative, or political—[in which] they need representation.

Thus, regrettably, the Kerr-Hayes encounter brought no composition of the issues involved. As not infrequently happens, labor and the intellectual somehow failed to make mental contact. This is particularly unfortunate at a time when so much depends on their mutual understanding. And specifically, so far as the Labor Reform Act is concerned, communication between labor and persons friendly to labor in the professional and academic world may make the difference between whether the LMRDA, whose grave deficiencies were discussed in Chapter 3, will function poorly, fairly well, or not at all. The courts and administrative agencies, upon whom implementation of the Act depends, will, logically enough, watch public opinion and react, as they generally do, to the greater pressures.

If nobody seems to care, they will, in the abiding tradition of bureaucrats everywhere, hope the problems will go away; a do-nothing attitude can easily develop. The standard operating policy of most public servants, after all, is the less action, the least error. Those who prefer the rather unsafe life of decision-making are not frequently encountered in government hierarchies.

The Kerr-Hayes exchange which so sadly misfired pointed up crucial areas in union democracy, some of which came to a head in the 1960s, and some of which are heading for resolution in the 1970s, if only because a *modus vivendi* must be found, and soon, given the great and growing power of the unions, the corporations, and the government, all of which threaten individual liberties on a broader scale (affecting virtually the whole population) than they have ever before been threatened in this nation.

The uses of power, union security, and the operation of internal union democracy are the key issues on which Kerr and Hayes failed to understand each other; and if these two men failed so signally, it is natural to wonder who can succeed. This sad conjecture in no way lessens the urgency of the task; it does underscore its inherent difficulties and the fact that the Kerr-Hayes debate of so many years ago is unfortunately intensely pertinent to developments in the 1970s and the Rubicon that labor cannot evade before that decade ends.

Dr. Kerr's proposal that unions recede from their broad activities beyond strictly industrial relations proceeds from the philosophically tenable premise that in this age of bigness power is evil, and the less there is of it, the better for individual freedom (a position with which Lord Acton and Bertrand Russell would not have quarreled). But labor leaders and rank-and-filers alike will strenuously dissent. That dissent is, of course, in no wise theoretic; it is rooted in the reality of union life. Labor necessarily views power accumulation as the *sine qua non* of unionism. Without power the unions of course could never achieve any of their goals, let alone even engage in the struggle for positive results at the bargaining table, or for influence and weight in Washington and the state capitals. Unionists view power not as an abstraction nor as a moral issue, but as an instrumentality.

Accordingly today few unionists, if any, would regard as helpful a return to the limited pure-and-simple unionism fathered by Samuel Gompers (at that, with tongue-in-cheek) and so carefully nurtured by the Wisconsin University labor theorists and their followers. That kind of two-by-four shopkeepers' unionism is as dead as the proverbial doornail and in fact never really existed, even when it was most ardently proclaimed as a theory of labor. Broad inclusive unionism is both the reality of the day and the condition of survival for the labor movement.

Both the leaders and the members generally consider that gains resulting from the union's "extracurricular" activities outweigh any loss of decision-making power about such details as determining where to locate a union-sponsored health clinic or housing project, or how to run a bank or recreational facilities. Neither members nor leaders are very knowledgeable in these areas. The accepted practice is to hire an expert. But while labor regularly uses the services of outsiders as paid consultants, technicians, administrators, and managers in organizing housing, health services, and other such sideline activities, and although labor people are generally unskilled in the use of abstract concepts, they are quite ready to pit their pragmatic experience against generalizations like those advanced by Dr. Kerr, including the claim that "union paternalism [such as] housing projects, vacation resorts, recreation facilities, has little more to recommend it than employer paternalism."

The union members know better. The miners would rather have their union paternalism with all its abuses and also all its benefits—medical services, retirement plans, welfare payments—than anything their employers ever did for them. The only kind of employer "paternalism" they ever experienced was company-supplied crutches at a price and cemeteries on company real estate.

The ladies garment and men's clothing workers similarly would not give up their health clinics, vacation resorts, cooperative housing, credit unions, and other manifestations of "union paternalism" even though they have no voice in decisions about the organization and operation of these facilities. Before the union launched such accommodations, the sweatshop was the only kind of "employer paternalism" these workers knew. With appropriate variations, the steel, electrical, automotive and other well-organized workers will all heartily join in this pragmatic acquiescence.

Surely there must be other and better ways to stimulate democracy in the unions than to escort them back to the far side of the railroad tracks of national life.

Not unrelated to the problem of union democracy is the problem of union security, a subject on which the labor leaders and their friends in the universities again have quite differing views. The intellectuals are inclined to assume that a union's present power is a reliable measure of its all-time potential. But as labor people know firsthand, any current level of a union's power reservoir is not a dependable basis for estimating future power reserves, which are subject to change without notice. Today's strength can be tomorrow's impotence; the reverse is true, too. The preponderance of variables over constants in labor experience creates a need to be prepared always for an uncertain future. The value of a union's bank reserves, signed contracts with management, established public prestige, and all the insignia of victory can be altered without advance warning by such powerful variables as the mood of the members, of the employers, or of the public; new inventions or production methods; changing economic circumstances in the nation, in an industry, indeed even in a single enterprise. Then too, and highly influential, are changing political and legislative climates, wars, the threat of war, and even the threat of peace breaking out in a defense-geared economy.

Of late new factors, such as the development of multi-national corporations, automation and changes in the complexion of the labor force, the shift of membership gravity from blue-collar to white-collar workers and the massive entry of women into industry in permanent as well as temporary jobs are defying all organizing calculations and planning.

True enough, unionism as a whole appears to be fairly well "established" and pretty generally "accepted," but individual unions are vulnerable, very much so. This may seem contradictory: If the parts are uncertain how can the whole be secure? But the paradox is solved once the proposition is accepted that the whole of unionism is bigger than the sum of its parts. Unionism is a component to be reckoned with in the nation's contemporary power structure and a central constituent of America in the making. In this sense (barring a totalitarian take-over) it can be considered practically indestructible. But individually even the strongest union may find itself fighting for its life despite its own power, relative opulence, and membership loyalty.

The miners' union is a case in point. The coal diggers' loyalty to their union is second to none. The "money worth" of an individual miner (his hypothetical share in the national union's treasury) is seven times more than that of a member of any of America's three biggest, most powerful unions—the teamsters, auto workers, and steel workers. But due to mechanization and the competition of other fuels with coal, the United Mine Workers of America is a shadow of its former self: three out of four miners are permanently disemployable in mining. District 50 of the UMWA may be netting in thousands of chemical workers, some stray office workers here and there, kitchen help, and other workers in unrelated fields, but none of that will ever add up to the great miners' union of only yesterday. No mine leader today is in a position to repeat John L. Lewis's arrogant challenge to the operators and the United States Government: "I hold labor in the palm of my hand; what am I bid?" Without in any way defending the appalling psychology behind the statement, its power is self-evident; but that power went more swiftly than it came.

Another type of difficulty, even danger, of playing safe in the union field is exemplified by the recent history of the well-established International Ladies Garment Workers' Union. David Dubinsky's heirs have to worry, among other concerns, about how to invest profitably and safely the general fund and reserves of the pension, health, and benefit funds, approximately a quarter of a billion dollars. But while the union reported an enrollment of 184,778 new members over a three-year period, there were some 2000 fewer members by the end of the period than at its start. Large and growing turnover is a peculiarity of this particular industry.

The miners' and the garment workers' problems are only two examples of why union security rests only in being ready for the unexpected. And other unions in other industries face other and no less-serious problems in reconciling the uncertainties of union life with the imperatives of internal union democracy.

Of all segments of society, labor lives closest to the edge of the volcano now threatening to erupt over the whole American landscape. In the circumstances any assumption that ignores the inherent precariousness of union life and proceeds from the simplistic basis that the unions have "arrived," are "established," and should therefore do thus and so, not unnaturally irritates even the most dynamic leaders. They are no less affronted than are the intellectuals when their seemingly logical and pertinent proposals are sometimes taken with a large handful of salt by tough-minded labor people.

The inescapable hard fact of labor life is that union power can never be taken for granted without the risk of grave miscalculation. Of course unions must take chances if they propose to survive and make headway. Even the most sheltered life is always a gamble. But labor leaders, both as practical politicians, which they are in the nature of their calling, and as responsible men on whom the fate of many thousands and even millions daily depends, must ever and continuously be taking stock of how much power they can mobilize in an emergency and accordingly determine just what their organizations want to do and what they can, in terms of reality, do successfully. The men who head the United Automobile Workers or the Steelworkers unions must trim their plans and materialize their ideas in part rather than "go for broke" and have General Motors and U.S. Steel accord their unions a state funeral. This makes for a certain conservatism in the leadership.

It is true that some union leaders exploit the security factor to insulate their personal hold on power against any and all criticism or needed reform of the internal democratic structure. "The fatherland is in danger" is a rallying cry for stifling dissent and moving patriots in the union as elsewhere; there, too, as in the larger community, patriotism is both the scoundrel's last refuge and also the honest democrat's prime duty.

Against this background, sidewalk superintendents of the union building process would do well to bear in mind the abiding insecurity of union power if they want to be listened to with respect by the people who are doing the building. It was Kerr's blind spot in excluding what might be called the unions' built-in vulnerability factor that provoked Hayes' impatience and made it not entirely unjustified. And in the years since their rather historic exchange (a historicity which a decade later seems to have escaped the attention of most labor historians) events gave added weight to the Hayes contention. Those events amply demonstrated that the unions had not then and never would "arrive" at that state of virtually impregnable power assumed by Kerr.

Among the many eloquent happenings in labor life that supported the Hayes thesis soon after it was set forth were the 116-day steel strike of 1959; the 1960 General Electric Company conflict with the union, preceded by the bitter, protracted Westinghouse strike, and the explosive three-year Henderson textile contest which ended in a union defeat. Then, not to be forgotten, there was the six-year Kohler Company fight against the UAW, during which the National Labor Relations Board charged Kohler with unfair labor practices and which in the end was won only by a miracle of union tenacity and solidarity. Nor can the general, unremitting, and still obtaining antagonism to unionization in the South be dismissed as merely a matter of climatic indisposition. And going a little farther south, just over the border, there are the dual American plants thriving on cheap Mexican labor.

Even more illustrative of the extent of general "acceptance" of unionism and its continuing vulnerability are the following two statements. One came from Joseph C. Bevis, board chairman of the Opinion Research Corporation of Princeton, in a report to the annual conference of the U.S. Chamber of Commerce in 1961. Said Mr. Bevis:

73% of the public across the nation agree that unions are necessary to protect the working men. 15% disagree, and 12% have no opinion. . . . Even among the owners and managers of business firms, 62% feel unions are necessary protection.

How deeply that prevailing acceptance is rooted in the minds of the shakers and makers of public opinion, which counts in nearly every final showdown, was underscored at the time by Massachusetts State Senator Francis X. McCann. Speaking on the Senate floor, as reported in the WEA News Report, he disclosed that:

. . . out of 1,726 newspapers in the United States, only 344 gave publicity to the recent anti-trust indictment of the General Electric Company, but . . . the misdeeds of a labor union [were] . . . publicized by 1,600 daily newspapers.

After all these years there appears to be continuing merit in the advice offered to labor when the unions were at peak power, back in 1951, by a *Life* editorial, "Labor View From A Plateau," which said:

. . . as an organ of democracy, the union movement has an agenda as long as democracy's own. It has no reason to be afraid, still less reason to relax.

The third and perhaps most disturbing issue over which many intellectuals and labor people fail to understand each other concerns the problem of how to protect a union member's right to dissent. Not many unions are in favor of setting up voluntary public review boards composed of outsiders. Union leaders may, of course, ultimately have second thoughts on the subject, if the present law is enforced, since it would compel them to submit to involuntary settlement of conflicts by the courts.

It is highly dubious, however, that any union would underwrite Dr. Kerr's proposal for a permanently functioning opposition party. He apparently assumes that there would never be a shortage of reasons for opposing the officers in power nor a dearth of issues. Perhaps people are too wicked to allow for a "nothing to complain about" situation ever occurring in union reality. Yet in scores of unions, national officers have served over long time spans without resort to dictatorial iniquity and muzzling of responsible dissent. It is not unthinkable that in one union or another there might just not be any need, for years on end, for a sustained opposition party. What would an opposition party do with itself without real "trouble" to live by? Might not its purposeless existence tend to breed the trouble necessary for its *raison d'être?*

"Actors standing in the wings and waiting to be called on," when and where there is no call and none is anticipated, could become a waiting invitation to corruption. The "ins" might be inclined to pay their worth in administrative jobs. And union-allergic employers might rate their value even higher and be prepared to subsidize the "outs" accordingly.

An oppositionary faction without a real issue can be no less detrimental to union democracy than an administration in power, no matter how otherwise worthy, that stifles reasonable, intelligent dissent. In terms of union reality, the need is not for a permanent opposition party but for competent, impartial machinery to help an honest opposition secure sensible, fair solutions of genuine conflicts, and to correct faulty conditions within the union that engender such conflicts.

Union leaders' thinking on this score rests, with rare exceptions, on a self-serving notion that what is good for the union is generally also morally good and, further, absolutely good for everyone in the union, an attitude based on too close an identification of the organization, that is, the operating hard core of the union, with the union *in toto.* But there are differences; some of these will be suggested and examined in the following chapter.

And there is, also, a public interest which at times transcends the interest of any particular segment of the population, even when it is as numerically large and vitally important as the union movement. As stated earlier, the union as a whole is more than the sum of its organizations. The nation, too, is more than the sum of the sectors that comprise it.

Even as American democratic society can no longer function as a representative government in the old way, union democracy too has burst the seams that contained it in the age of the town meeting. The extraordinary upsurge of unionism in the last generation, the power which unions have built up and the tenacity which they demonstrate, as well as the resistances they are now facing, make the old union folklore of internal procedures dated and insufficient.

Beyond question the state of the unions' internal democratic operations are in need of repair. Any mending, however, must consider the actualities of the union movement and the directions in which it is moving, together with the thrust of national developments, or the mending will harm, not help.

5

DEMOCRACY IN ACTION
PART ONE

The International Longshoremen's Association
The International Brotherhood of Longshoremen
The United Brotherhood of Carpenters & Joiners

As indicated in the previous chapter, any serious effort to correct the failings of union democracy must carefully consider whether a proposed remedy will be helpful or injurious. It is advisable also to know the patient, his functional behavior and peculiarities, recuperative capacities and past history. Additionally, a due respect for the organism itself and a proper awareness of the limitations of therapy are helpful in avoiding blunders that can sometimes be fatal.

The organism here under discussion is the labor movement, that sector of the body politic-socioeconomic, which in the view of so many is so very ill. Its leadership and internal democratic processes do not seem to be functioning as well as they might. But perhaps they are functioning as well as they can in a national and world situation that is truly pathological. The possibility, at least, should not be entirely excluded, nor should the fact that the patient has issued no loud complaints.

But without embarking on a fruitless discussion of who is sick and who sicker, perhaps it would be useful to consider that the overuse or overkill of medical weaponry has itself produced so many devastating side effects that there is now a category of new, doctor-induced diseases. Attention is called to these iatrogenic ailments lest a similar fate befall the labor movement, for whose real and imagined ills there already exists a plethora of proposed remedies. Some are on the statute books, some on the drafting boards of labor-management consulting firms, some in academic textbooks, and some flowing free in the slightly jaundiced view of the unions expounded in some university courses, in editorials, and articles by learned men.

This brief excursion into pharmacology and physicians is not directed by a congenital aversion to either one (some of this writer's best friends are doctors) but by a dislike for the medical profession as a business enterprise and as a cautionary word to those seriously concerned with the ills of the labor segment of society.

Since past events sometimes have a stronger impact on current developments than more clearly visible contemporary happenings whose real effects cannot in fact be gauged until some time has elapsed, the following pages focus on three distinct situations that helped shape the 1960s, offering lessons still largely unlearned as the decade moved to an end and therefore of even added importance for the union learning process in the 1970s:

The three situations discussed in this chapter and the next are viewed both in close-up and also from a decade's perspective. One involved an attempt that failed, using democratic methods, to free a major union from underworld control. The two others indicate how inextricably intertwined in union reality are the problems of leadership, power, and democracy as they meet, head-on, at the conventions of powerful unions.

Do Members Want a Clean Union?—ILA

In 1953 the AFL, then not yet merged with the CIO, attempted at its convention in St. Louis to wrest control of the International Longshoremen's Association from the corrupt leadership which had for years ruled the waterfront. National leaders of the ILA and officers of its New York and surrounding subdivisions had been exposed by the New York State Crime Commission as corrupt, linked with and largely dominated by the criminal underworld. The struggle began with the expulsion of the

ILA from the Federation. This drastic measure was pushed through at the convention by George Meany, who had become AFL President that year and who simply would not tolerate corruption in the union movement. The action, of course, ran counter to the long-standing policy of nonintervention by the Federation's Executive Council in the internal affairs of its affiliates.

Following the ILA's expulsion, the AFL launched a new union, the International Brotherhood of Longshoremen, under responsible, decent union leadership. Sizable funds were allocated and organizers delegated in an effort to persuade ILA members to quit the crime-infested union and join up with the new IBL. The response was at best inconclusive. The AFL-sponsored union lost out to the corrupt old crowd in two consecutive elections conducted in 1953 and 1954 by the National Labor Relations Board to determine which union the longshoremen wanted to represent them. The vote was heavy, although not all eligibles voted. In the first election, 9060 voted for ILA membership and 7568 for the IBL. There were also 4399 votes challenged, mainly by the AFL. Because of violence and intimidation at the polls, the NLRB cancelled the election results.

The score in the subsequent election was 9110 for the ILA and 8871 for the IBL; there were 1797 challenged votes, mostly by the AFL union. The Board decision, following this second vote, unavoidably went to the gangster-run ILA. The latter then secured a two-year union-shop contract from the shipowners. The battle was lost, the war continued for two years, and then a new test was made in a third NLRB election, in October 1956. Again the majority favored the ILA, which received 11,827 votes to 7428 for the AFL-sponsored IBL.

Did the NLRB elections prove that the majority of the longshoremen actually wanted racketeers to run their union?

In a study of waterfront labor, sociologist Daniel Bell suggested that "roughly about one-third of the men" favored the crooked union in which "they had considerable privileges because of the system of favoritism. This group worked hard for the ILA." Their privileges included better jobs, better treatment on the job, and steadier employment than other longshoremen had. Perhaps those so favored had special skills or were ready to use them for special services; perhaps they had good "connections" or were influential in their respective groups; perhaps they also had police records. But whatever their individual endowments or achievements, all had demonstrated at one time or another unswerving obedience to orders, and that was what counted most to the officers.

The ILA did not operate in a vacuum; its officers needed support and cultivated it by according special privileges to strategic individuals and groups. And with their support in turn assured, the leaders could and did put the majority on the auction block. Minority control is of course not confined to crooked unionism, but in the violent setting of the New York waterfront terror can be a very persuasive argument. Many who abstained or voted ILA did so not through preference but through fear of revenge by the criminal contingent. Additionally, there was little confidence that the AFL meant business, that a new deal for the longshoremen was actually in the making. Experience argued against believing that this was more than a brawl between contending leaders for the spoils of office.

Such shaky confidence as existed was not bolstered by the fact that New York's then AFL chief, President Marty Lacey of the city Central Trades and Labor Council, had ruled out any discussion in that body of ILA issues. Nor did Teamster boss Dave Beck's prominent part in the AFL's expulsion of the ILA instill confidence in the outcome. These events preceded by three years Beck's own public fall from innocence: but if his union peers did not know it, ordinary folks already had no illusions about honesty in the teamsters' union and its high command. Skeptical longshoremen not unnaturally wondered why Mr. Beck did not clean up his own union first.

The almost 7500 votes polled by the AFL union in 1956 was a smaller percentage than it won in 1954. But in the two-year interval the number of men employed on the docks fell from 33,551 to 27,272. Numerically the vote in 1956 for the ILA was 2700 more than in 1954. A press report at the time indicated that votes for the ILA included some 4000 workers of various crafts employed on the waterfront whom the jurisdiction-conscious new AFL union would not touch. If true, this would show that the vote was in fact about even for the two contending unions. But such speculations aside, if the vote of almost 9000 for the IBL in

1954 was a measure of courage, the vote of close to 7500 in 1956 was a measure of faith, the kind which, in more propitious circumstances, moves mountains. Clearly, a substantial segment of the longshoremen—probably half of them—wanted a clean union. But did the leaders who appealed for their faith and courage want a clean union strongly enough to put up a real fight for it?

In the initial contest, the AFL spent $1,000,000 to gain the longshoremen's allegiance to oust the ILA. Having lost, the AFL-sponsored IBL held to its title and kept up a skeleton organization. It is true that the new union could not do much in the two years that the ILA had an agreement with shipping and stevedoring companies. But when the contract was over and a new contest was possible, the IBL was enabled to put into the field only one organizer and to publish a weekly newsletter to win the support of 27,000 longshoremen.

Had George Meany deserted the clean union he had launched just two years earlier? No indeed; he wrote a personal letter to each of the longshoremen. He stood by his guns; they just weren't loaded. Paul Hall, president of the Seafarers' International Union, helped. But on the eve of the NLRB election, Joseph Curran, president of the National Maritime Union, made public a letter to George Meany asking him to cancel his support of the International Brotherhood of Longshoremen, thus in effect supporting the underworld-controlled ILA. Did Mr. Curran love the corrupt ILA? No, but he loved the president of the Seafarers' union even less, a dislike based on jurisdictional competition. And of course there were the Teamsters' Dave Beck and Jimmy Hoffa supporting the ILA in hopes of taking it into their own organization. All these elements being actively present, it was no wonder that corruption won. Only in 1957 did the McClellan rackets investigating committee arrive on the scene to call a spade a spade.

Outside the AFL-CIO, the ubiquitous John L. Lewis handsomely put several hundred thousand dollars of the United Mine Workers' funds at the disposal of the crooked ILA to help tide over its financial troubles. Did Lewis love the racketeers? Not at all. His own union at that time had never been scandal-tainted. But he hated the AFL, and it was amusing to cause it trouble.

There were other similar high-order multimotivated interventions by the men on labor's Olympus and below. The result was that the clean union went with the wind. Under the circumstances, the fact that nearly 7500 longshoremen dared vote in 1956 against gangs and corruption was a miracle of the waterfront, and no orchids to the union movement. Out of fear and considerations of job security, it is human and understandable that half of the longshoremen voted for the corrupt *status quo*. Majorities in every congregation of men consider their own safety first. It is often the task of intelligent, courageous minorities to save the majorities from themselves.

Machine Rule and Guts
(The United Brotherhood of Carpenters & Joiners)

Maurice A. Hutcheson, President of the United Brotherhood of Carpenters and Joiners, had inherited his rule of "an empire in wood" from his father, William Hutcheson, and so, although an election of officers was on the agenda of the union's 1958 convention in St. Louis, the union's top executive was not overly concerned. As longtime heir apparent he had come to expect the best, even in a sometimes wicked world.

Nepotism exists in the unions as elsewhere. It is natural for fathers to seek to give their sons a good start in life. And if the son wishes to follow in his father's well-heeled footsteps, that too is understandable and in fact sometimes praiseworthy, as is the fact that such a son's devotion does not necessarily end at the graveside. Moreover if, as in the case of the Carpenters' ruling dynasty, the son decides to perpetuate his father's revered name by commissioning a biography about him—a literary monument, as it were—union members, unlike Senate snoops, will not question the display of filial affection involved, even if it costs money, a lot of money. The carpenters were earning well and they had not objected to footing the bill. Unfortunately others—"outsiders," naturally—had. They had created a problem which the Carpenters' president did not seek to evade.

Maurice A. Hutcheson opened the Carpenters Convention with an account of the many harassments to which he had been subjected by the United States Senate Rackets Investigating Committee. Not least among them were the unfavorable repercussions from the publishing project that had been conceived as a memorial to his father, the Carpenters' deceased president and great, dedicated leader. The union had engaged a writer, one Maxwell Raddock, to prepare, print, and distribute a biography of the late William Hutcheson. Mr. Raddock had received $50,000 to do the necessary research. As publisher and distributor, Mr. Raddock, it was brought out by the McClellan investigation, had also netted a profit of $185,000, rather more than the average best-seller makes, and for all Hutcheson's manifest virtues, his biography was obviously not in that category. The McClellan Committee had cast doubt on the honesty and/or competence of the officers in this affair.

When called to testify, Maurice Hutcheson had not invoked the Fifth Amendment; he had simply refused to answer. A charge of contempt was filed against him. The McClellan Committee had then dug up an old charge that the late Hutcheson had appropriated from the union 200 shares of the profitable stock of the Adams Fruit Company of Florida, a corporation linked with the citrus fruit operations of the Carpenters' Home for Old Members in Florida. The Senatorial Committee wanted the facts and figures.

And apart from all this the son had his own troubles. An Indiana State court had indicted Maurice Hutcheson and two other national officers for having participated in a five-way split of an $80,000 profit on right-of-way land sales for use in a Federal-aided highway system; in consequence the United States Senate Public Lands Subcommittee was questioning Mr. Hutcheson and investigating the matter.

All these harassments were laid at the door of "the enemies of labor" in the report submitted by President Hutcheson to the convention. The report closed with this plea:

> Like all other human beings, I may have made mistakes, but I believe that they have been of the head and not of the heart, because my heart has always been with the Brotherhood and you, its beloved members. It always will be. I have served you in the ranks; and in whatever posi-

tion I have held or may hold, I regard myself as always
serving in the ranks.

Mr. Hutcheson's personal statement was received with the
usual loud applause, was unanimously approved, and made an official part of the Officers' Report.

It was impossible to tell whether the delegates appreciated
their president's lifelessly delivered address. The cheers and hand-
clapping seemed perfunctory. Having observed a great many union
conventions, this writer does not recall having witnessed any other
so unconcerned with the politics of its top-level officers.

Conversations with several of the carpenters revealed them
to be a rather alert, lively group. When one of the Southern District officers was asked if the delegates were concerned with their
national officers' extraordinary activities, the answer was, "We're
concerned with making a living; they don't interfere and they
don't like to be interfered with, and that's the size of it." He
introduced the writer to some delegates who were passing by,
among them two Negroes, emphasizing that there was a friendly
good fellowship, color or no, and they were all seemingly satisfied with the convention.

The delegates seemed animated enough in the lobbies, bars, in
the streets walking to and from the convention hall, but they
were virtually impassive during the actual sessions, paying practically no attention to the procedures on stage. To formal calls
from the Chair: "Those in favor say Aye, contrary-minded No,"
the usual response was a few hardly audible voices. Of course
there was the proper show of enthusiasm when the occasion demanded, although no chances were taken with spontaneity. The
necessary paraphernalia of noisemaking were prepared in advance, as in most union conventions. The delegates took their
president's ethics "of the heart" in their stride.

A prominent New York lawyer and one-time candidate of
the Republican party for Governor who was counsel for the
Brotherhood undertook to allay any possible misgivings. He ex-
plained that the Raddock book had used many pictures, and that
their reproduction was costly. As to the Indiana case, that was

nothing to fret about since, until and unless convicted, a man must be considered innocent. The attack on the hallowed memory of the senior Hutcheson was another matter, since the great leader was gone and could no longer defend himself. To that end the Brotherhood's counsel quoted the opinion of the Honorable Horner C. Fisher, a Florida lawyer and ex-President of the Florida Bar Association, who had personally investigated the charges of alleged appropriation of 200 shares of the Adams Company stock, presumably union property. In the opinion of the Honorable Mr. Fisher:

> The accusation against the late president is at best a stale one, which should not recommend itself to a court of equity and good conscience after the lapse of so many years, the death of so many people, the closing of so many lips, and the loss or disappearance of so much evidence that might have been available many years ago.

To these wise words the union's own counsel added his eloquent recommendation:

> Thus Mr. Fisher is advising you that, when Time has sealed the evidence in the grave, the law will not use conjecture as a spade to exhume and dishonor the bones of dead men.

In plain talk, it was a case of falling back on the helpful statute of limitations, but the delegates were treated to some 45 minutes of purple prose and the least they could do in response was to give the speaker the standard "standing ovation."

A convention committee, on the second day of meetings, reported resolutions from thirteen district and state organizations representing the bulk of the membership, which called on the convention to express appreciation of the officers' work and "to retain them." The committee recommended that the convention concur. At that point the unexpected happened: not ethics, but democracy showed up. A delegate rose to question the whole procedure. He said that adoption of the report would render meaningless the nominations of officers, which was to be held the next day. The chairman called for a vote. The voice vote was uncertain and the presiding officer asked for a show of hands, after which he declared the motion to retain the officers had passed. There was a rumble of dissatisfaction and requests for a roll-call vote. Mr. Hutcheson, who was not presiding over the session, intervened. There was point to objection from the floor, he acknowledged. The matter was then dropped, no further voting seemed in order, and the chairman went on to other business.

But trouble surged back the next day during the nominations. A delegate from a California local arose to place in nomination one E. A. Brown, the preceding day's objector, as candidate for membership on the General Executive Board, characterizing his candidate in these words:

> . . . a real man, an honest man, a man with guts . . . He was the first man who stood up here yesterday afternoon and expressed an opinion, an opinion of many, many people in this auditorium. He was the first man who has had guts to express an opinion. This man has been doing this sort of thing in the California State Council of Carpenters for many years. He has taken a lot of bruises, but he has always stood for what is right and he has always stood for principles. . . . He has supported the working man . . . in the face of apathy, in the face of appeasement, in the face of the sit-down-and-do-nothing sort of thing that we have seen entirely too much of.

Two more delegates nominated Brown, each again stressing his guts. But Mr. Brown did not get beyond the honor of being nominated from the floor. For the General Executive Board consists of district directors who are named in caucus meetings, and customarily the convention merely confirms the caucus nominees. Thus Mr. Brown remained with his "guts" but no seat on the

General Board. Yet for many there had been, if only briefly, an almost reassuring sound of storm in the stifling vapors of the seemingly unchanging regulation convention-hall atmosphere.

Hutcheson and the other top officers were, as expected, elected unanimously. In each instance there was only one nomination, and the presiding officer would routinely declare: "I therefore instruct the Secretary to cast a unanimous ballot for . . . ," and the masquerade of democracy proceeded, apparently harmless and unharmed, as in so many unions.

The convention devoted considerable time to the interrelated problems of jurisdiction and of technological changes which were already eating into the old skills and creating demands for new skills. William F. Patterson, then Special Assistant to the Secretary of Labor, told the delegates:

> . . . Total construction expenditures, including maintenance and repair, rose from $20 billion in 1946 to $60 billion in 1956. By 1966, constant dollar expenditures for new construction, maintenance and repair may reach $85 billion . . . The rate of employment increase for building-trades craftsmen—24 per cent—is expected to be greater than the average rate of growth for skilled occupations.

The burden of the message was that the union must do its utmost to catch up with changing skills; but it also implicitly highlighted the carpenters' need to meet the shift of work to the jurisdictions of other unions as technological changes in the work process were taking place. All this led finally to the adoption of a resolution authorizing the General Executive Board to withdraw the union from the AFL-CIO at its discretion.

This resolution was adopted in a most unusual way. It first appeared as a printed document with some 50 signatures; this was then circulated for more names from the start of the convention until the morning of the third day, by which time it had 1156 signatures. Only then was the resolution presented; it was carried almost unanimously, with only two dissenting votes.

President Hutcheson assured the delegates that withdrawal

from the AFL-CIO would be the very last resort in the union's defense against jurisdictional invasion.

The danger that such defense might be needed was indicated by the incursions which the industrial unions, it was claimed, were making into the carpenters' jurisdictional field, and which the AFL-CIO high command had thus far failed to arrest. This ground had been well covered and heavily stressed before the resolution authorizing possible withdrawal from the merged Federation was presented. Although the delegates had voted overwhelmingly for it, there were few present who did not know that a little problem of "ethics" was much involved in the threat to quit the AFL-CIO. George Meany, its president, was embarrassingly insistent that Mr. Hutcheson, a vice-president of the Federation, account for his financial manipulations to his peers in some clear way.

The Brotherhood high command had obviously decided that they would rather take their union out of the AFL-CIO than face the onus of expulsion or go into explanations about Mr. Hutcheson's "head and heart." As to the members, they just as obviously accepted that the union administration was a power beyond their reach and that nothing could be done about it. At least not then. One try had been made. Everyone felt a bit more virtuous for the attempt to seat a candidate not backed by the machine on the GEB. And who knew if E. A. Brown would have exhibited as much democratic "guts" as a board member as he had displayed in his effort to become one? After all, the union did provide for good work terms and pay; practical men put first things first.

And finally, the Carpenters' convention refused to accept the then recently adopted AFL-CIO Code of Ethical Practices—a gesture that spoke for itself.

As footnote to the whole affair, the United Brotherhood of Carpenters and Joiners is still an AFL-CIO affiliate, and Maurice A. Hutcheson is still its reigning president.

6

DEMOCRACY IN ACTION
PART TWO

The United Steelworkers of America in Convention

Three prominent guest speakers addressed the United Steelworkers Union 1958 Convention in Atlantic City—former President Harry S. Truman; future President John F. Kennedy, then the junior Senator from Massachusetts; and James P. Mitchell, then Secretary of Labor.

"This kind of meeting is in essence an example of democracy in America," said Secretary Mitchell.

Senator Kennedy joined in the praise: "I wish my Democratic colleagues in the Senate could see this democratic union convention in action." Former President Truman was equally generous. The three speakers were knowledgeable men and what they said was largely true. The USWA is a democratic union.

But in the course of this convention "democracy in action" was given such a strenuous workout as to raise serious questions about the viability of traditional modes of internal union democracy in situations of severe stress. Six of the nine convention sessions were, for the most part, conducted in a businesslike manner by obviously serious people performing in the tradition of progressive, broadly inclusive unionism characteristic of the CIO orientation and operation.

The Officers' report and the various resolutions presented by local unions for action by the convention offered an impressive array of material and of mature thinking on matters of importance to the union, such as:

Steelworkers and the national economy; agreements, cost of living, wages, arbitration, benefits;

Finances, social insurance, pensions;

Legislation, national and in the states, in the courts, the NLRB, civil rights;

Ethical practices—codes and processing;

International affairs, general and labor;

Union departments—health, research, education, housing, etc.

Decisions subsequently reached covered a no less impressive range of topics of concern to the members as workers in the industry and as citizens in the nation.

The delegates listened attentively, spoke rarely but to the point when a facet of any issue was close to home, and voted on all these matters nearly always unanimously.

Ethics, strictly speaking, was not at issue in this convention. Democracy was. In three stormy sessions that vividly contrasted with the orderly proceedings of the sessions mentioned above, the contenders believed, or at least claimed to believe, that a basic principle of democratic union government was at stake.

The administration, supported by 98 percent of the convention's 3550 delegates, fought with the determination worthy of a great cause against a handful of men about what was, in fact, a minor issue. On the face of things, at issue was an amendment to the union's constitution presented by several local unions and supported by the opposition. They proposed that union agents and representatives who service the local organizations or act as organizers, staff men, as they are called in the USWA, be elected to office by the members in the local unions and serve under local authority.

In the prevailing system, these staff men are appointed by the union's general president under the reviewing authority of the International Executive Board, which usually also proposes the names of appointees. The proposed amendment would have reduced the power of the directors of some 30 districts who constitute the International Executive Board.

The people involved in the battle that ensued were David J. McDonald who was then union president, and McKeesport furnace tender Donald C. Rarick, leader of the opposition. Rarick had had the effrontery, six months earlier, to challenge Mr. Mc-

Donald for the USWA presidency and had polled the amazing total of 223,516 votes against McDonald's 404,172 votes in a nationwide referendum.

Now the union upstart was again challenging the union president.

The Executive Board's opposition to the amendment could have been anticipated; the Board was supported in resolutions from 80 local unions. The fact is that the issue did not seem to evoke major interest in the local units; in all only 93 resolutions pro and con were presented, as contrasted with 500 local resolutions on wage-policy matters. (In a more routine situation the disparity would not be striking, since unionists, like most people, are more concerned with earnings than with organization politics.) But the agitation on both sides of this internal contest could have been expected to produce somewhat more substantial interest in the proposed reform.

Furthermore, within the small number of interested local unions, the proponents of the Rarick amendment were a minority of one to six. After the stormiest and bitterest encounter in the convention the vote stood 50 for the Rarick proposals and 3528 for the administration. The union constitution was obviously in no danger from the reformers.

The wrath of the union leaders was directed against Rarick not as the proponent of several anti-administration resolutions in 1958 that had no support to speak of but against Rarick as the upstart president of a McKeesport local union of several thousand members, a political nobody who had caused Mr. McDonald a humiliating loss of face a half year earlier by daring to run for the presidency. True enough, Rarick had been beaten. McDonald had been reelected by a better than 64 percent majority. An Eisenhower or Roosevelt might be happy with a 55 percent majority; not so union presidents. They are accustomed to having majorities of at least 85 or 90 percent. (Still better, of course, is no opposing candidate at all.)

The convention battle was meaningful not because it exposed the weakness of the opposition but because it threw light on certain weaknesses in the operations of union majorities, and not only among the steelworkers. These weaknesses are a facet, ten years later, of the contemporary union reality and consequently merit consideration. It may seem captious to stress a solitary unhappy event in the steelworkers' convention, since the union itself is one of the outstandingly progressive and constructive labor organizations in the nation; but the USWA is a union to which many look with hope and for guidance. In such circumstances, disappointments are particularly painful.

Rarick's bid for presidency of the USWA had had its origins two years earlier, at the 1956 convention in Los Angeles. That convention met soon after the settlement of a steel strike which was then hailed, despite some dissenting voices, as "the greatest gain ever." Not too wisely, but not unnaturally, the union administration chose the occasion to present proposals for raising the officers' salaries, with President McDonald's annual pay to be bettered from 40,000 to 50,000 dollars. The convention showed little enthusiasm for the proposal, and much of that thinned to the vanishing point when, right after the proposed salary increases, a move was made to increase dues payments from 3 dollars to 5 dollars a month.

It is not uncommon to couple proposals to increase officers' pay with a good-looking improvement in workers' pay. This is a logical consequence of the "more" concept of unionism. A measure of improvement is meted out to some according to their simple tastes, to others according to their exalted status. The 50,000 dollar figure, identified as just reward for McDonald's labor, was not out of line. John L. Lewis, Daniel Tobin, Dave Beck and many others were already in the 50,000 dollar bracket. And closely approaching it were the Musicians' Petrillo, the Railway Clerks' Harrison, the Carpenters' Hutcheson, to mention only a few. Labor leaders follow without too much resistance the "better yourself" trend of management.

At the steelworkers' convention, habitual practice hit a snag. It might have been avoided if time had been allowed to elapse between salary raises and dues increases. But coming together as they did, they caused an uproar. Some simply disliked the prospect of paying higher dues, just as their employers dislike paying higher taxes. Others, lacking the requisite experience, failed to appreciate how difficult it may be for a union president to make ends meet on only 40,000 dollars a year, taxes and new social obligations considered.

It may be noted, in fairness to some who merit it, that the featured recipient of a substantial salary increment is not necessarily the villain of the piece. He may well be the figurehead in an action for which he personally has no stomach. For example, one union president in private talk with this writer said when he was advised that an upcoming convention would "demand" that his salary be substantially increased:

> What do I want this increase for? With pretty much every reasonable expense of mine paid by the union, my salary is comfortably sufficient.

In the end the union president took the raise after all. He had to "work with his people." The driving force back of most demands for pay increases to top officers, although presented as an effort to "equate compensation with the responsibility of office," often has more realistic overtones. The salary increase for the top officer is a curtain raiser for increases down the union hierarchical line. Quite often the clamor for financial "justice" for "the great leader" comes from those who in turn will most benefit by that act of justice.

In any case, McDonald did not resist the pay increment. Perhaps he merely reacted as the "organization man" that he in fact was. Or he may very well have wanted a raise to support his rather expensive "high life." Whatever his motive, a reaction was set in motion. After the Chairman's gavel brought the stormy session of the 1956 convention to a close and the Chairman announced that "the ayes have it," meaning higher salaries and heavier dues, a number of delegates formed a Dues Protest Committee. The members of this committee later decided to challenge McDonald in the forthcoming referendum election of national officers, scheduled for February, 1957.

The polling of 223,516 votes in this referendum by Donald C. Rarick was, with the exception of the McClellan Committee disclosures, the most shattering event of the labor year. The pro-Rarick vote had in effect annulled union gravitational law. Rarick was unknown, he had no resources except what supporting members voluntarily chipped in, and his loose, spotty organization was held together only by the feeling of displeasure with McDonald. The union president, in contrast, had at his service the efficient and far-flung USWA machinery, with its well-organized publicity channels. And election finances were no problem; the union treasury was in good shape. Yet against these seemingly overwhelming odds Rarick and his supporters had administered a major political shiner to Dave McDonald and his administration. The latter were determined to prevent the Rarick opposition from entrenching itself on the basis of its near coup. The opposition in turn, having tasted blood, wanted more. Rarick had previously announced that, win or lose, his dues protest committee did not intend to disband:

> We intend to make sure our organization stays together. . . . We will start working at the local level.

Charges and countercharges came in rapid succession. The details were not edifying. Rarick filed charges with the McClellan Committee, accusing McDonald of having stolen the election, of spending a million dollars to bolster his incumbency. When no favorable action was taken by the Senate Committee, Rarick's attorney filed a one-million dollar lawsuit in a Pennsylvania court against the union and McDonald personally for false accusations, character assassination and the like. The McDonald people accused the opposition of the most heinous crime in the union book, "dual unionism." On neither side did the charges make sense.

The administration denied the charge that union funds were used to re-elect McDonald, which may have been technically true. The activities of the McDonald supporters, the union representatives and committee members, were automatically taken care of by the routine budget. No special funding was required as they boosted McDonald in their reports at local union or plant meetings, or at the various area conferences and chance get-togethers in bars. This was their accustomed duty. The union's monthly publication also performed its routine duty in supporting the administration. Identification of the organization with its officers is the governing law of all union operations. (The sole exception to this rule is the International Typographical Union's Journal which allows equal space to incumbent and opposition candidates in union elections.)

One of the several blunders made by Rarick's attorney, himself an ex-steelworker, was to ask for a court determination of whether USWA funds had been used to pay for McDonald's newspaper ads, and radio and TV time during the campaign. None of this publicity had mentioned the election or the opposition but had instead merely recapitulated membership benefits obtained during the McDonald administration.

Rarick failed to secure favorable action by the courts or the McClellan Committee. And the Committee's investigators were not blindfolded.

The charge that McDonald had stolen the election lacked substance. He didn't have to. True, there was widespread dissidence early in 1957 because of the upheaval over dues and salaries; otherwise Rarick would never have polled a quarter of a million votes. But while McDonald himself was not overwhelmingly popular, neither was the opposition. It would take a sturdier, more compelling figure than Rarick's, and one more skilled in organization politics, to rally the various groups who had never accepted McDonald in the first place or who had, for legitimate reasons, learned to like him less the more they knew him.

Such a man, I. W. Abel, took part in the various incidents described in this section. In all of them he supported McDonald. During, before, and after the 1958 convention, I. W. Abel was a key member of the McDonald administration. But he would have had to be blind to miss the lesson of Rarick's failure—that disaffection in the union was so great that even an amateur politician from McKeesport could roll up a quarter of a million protest votes against the union president. Rarick had tested the ground for an election that would, in 1965, mark McDonald's defeat and a resounding victory for I. W. Abel as president of the USWA.

But that is another story. At the time however, irritation over the dues increase subsided as increasing unemployment and disemployment due to technological causes made for sentiment against rocking the boat. The union had secured supplementary unemployment benefits for the members.

McDonald would never be a Phil Murray, but he had the support of a powerful organization, a certain synthetic prestige, and money. Thousands of subaltern union officers, committeemen, and workers in strategic positions in the plants, largely dependent on the local administration for favors and privileges, worked for the McDonald slate. Of course it is not entirely impossible that some pro-administration men had lent a clandestine hand to the Rarick dues-protest movement, not with a view to defeating McDonald but to shake him up a bit, to make him more fully aware of his need for the goodwill of intermediate echelons in the union's power apparatus. Such occasional strayings from the straight and narrow path by good men and true are not unknown in politics, in the unions as elsewhere.

The McDonald charge that the opposition was receiving money from anti-union employers was easy to make and hard to prove. It was natural that the ins should suspect the outs, and vice versa, especially in view of steel management's old trouble-making record of union infiltration. These practices may no longer exist, but their memories die hard. Union leaders still tend to see an employer's pocketbook back of any opposition. Where do they get the money? Surely they are not spending their own. Management dollars more than once have helped stir troubled union waters, but so far as the opposition in the USWA is concerned, in the years under discussion no one has yet produced a single fact to prove it.

What the administration people forgot was that a good many of them, in their younger, more innocent days, had performed endless unpaid work for the union; they had worked gladly, unsparingly, when the union itself was an "insurgency" against inimical employers. In those days they had not hesitated to spend "their own money," but now they refused to believe that the new rebels might be doing exactly the same thing.

The steelworkers always were a fighting lot. They had proved that back in the Homestead strike-lockout of 1892, and at least once in every decade since. In 1956 they were, by their own standards, prosperous and could afford to finance a good

scrap, which always appealed to them. But perhaps before return-
ing to some of the other none-too-pretty developments of the
USWA Convention in 1958, a look at the union's leadership,
background, and membership is in order.

The USWA is a young union, but by 1958 it had, after 20
years, made its way "from nothing yesterday to everything today."
The steelworkers pretty nearly had it "all" and were "everything" here and now. They knew they had built their union by
their own will, efforts, and fighting stamina; no officer or group
owned or could take it away from the members.

"Old timers" and the younger men among the 1958 convention delegates made no secret of their pride in the union's past.
The USWA story was writ large in blown-up photos and big
lettering on the quarter-mile-long walls along the ramp which
delegates and visitors traversed four times daily walking to and
from the convention auditorium. The panels graphically depicted
highlights of the war of liberation from the iron heel of the
steel companies. That war had been waged by the Steelworkers'
Organizing Committee set up by John L. Lewis in 1936 and led
by the unforgettable and beloved Philip Murray. In 1942 the
Committee was reorganized into the United Steelworkers of
America. Hitherto "alone, afraid, mute," the steelworkers emerged
mass-organized, finding friends and associates in the national labor
movement, and successfully battling for economic improvement
and citizenship in the industry.

Most of the delegates in '58 were in the prime of life. Their
past was not a vague recollection of bygones, but fresh, colorful
total recall of "only yesterday" and 1936, 1941 and 1950 were
vividly alive for almost all of them. Only the very young, of
whom there were just a few, may not have known from personal
experience or adolescent memories what a steelworker's life was
like when management's power was uncurbed, when the union
was practically non-existent, when a worker could only choke on
his own dissent, dislike, protest. Although the ability to forget is
at times a condition of survival, it can also be a cause of destruction. These people did not intend to forget.

Many remembered that their union, born in battle with the
steel barons, was also the by-product of a rebellion within the
union movement itself. Their own Phil Murray, together with

Lewis and a few other leaders, had set in motion the historic civil war against a do-nothing AFL leadership, which had grown stale, immobile, seemingly oblivious to the great changes then rapidly occurring in the economic and political world. It was in the course of that head-on collision of men and ideas that Lewis put forward the daring plan and mapped the brilliant strategy of the 1936 "grand design."

These were all events that shaped the special character of the steelworker. A fair characterization of the members of the union 20 years after it was founded, at the time of the 1958 convention, and which has hardly since altered, would include the following features:

The steelworkers, as a group, are consciously active unionists, with special pride in their past.

The highly centralized character of the industry and the corporate power and wealth concentrated in it, together with its over-all record of anti-unionism, has kept alive a certain militance among the members. It is significant, for example, that the rank-and-file never fell for Mr. McDonald's beloved "doctrine of mutual trusteeship" to be exercised by the top brass of the union and the steel corporations, which he so ardently tried to sell to the parties on both sides of the bargaining table.

Other significant characteristics of union members are the relatively high earnings and greatly improved working conditions achieved within two decades. These have enhanced the steelworker's feeling of self-respect and community status.

The in-plant or shop society is a pro-union activizing factor among the steelworkers; some 30,000 shop committeemen are stewards, serving as a liaison between the local unions and the mass of the workers. The steelworkers have a large number of active members. Among the 3550 delegates to the 1958 USWA convention, close to 1000 delegates were local union officers or representatives of the national organization assigned to local areas. When the opposition charged that the convention was packed with staffers, McDonald called on delegates who were staff members to stand up. Only 150 did. Hundreds of committeemen and shop stewards who were among the delegates did not. Such people tend to see eye-to-eye with the administration, an attitude not restricted to steelworkers. Delegates to union conventions are generally chosen by union members from those who know the union business best, who actively take part in local matters and are therefore equipped to serve as delegates.

Also, at least 2000, possibly 2500, local activists were present, who were not on the union payroll and had no national expense account to bolster their loyalty to the administration. It is of course entirely speculative whether any two thousand people can be truly representative of a million and a quarter workers in a union. But this problem exists in every representative body, not excluding the U.S. Congress. In democracies, the tail sometimes wags the dog.

The extent of active delegate participation in the convention's legislative work can be judged by the membership of the committees which processed all proposals from local unions and national leaders. Thus there were 65 on the Resolutions Committee; 61 on the Constitution, 55 on the Officers' Report, and 25 on the Appeals Committee, in all only 206 committee members. Unfortunately, their agendas were so crowded that the committees could do no more than follow the direction of the national leaders and the advice of the national organization's technicians.

In general this is the way all union conventions operate, and there may be no better way except for details of performance. The committees had to carry out their assignments in an environment of oratory, parades, the "great debate" on the opposition's resolutions and the decision on the opposition itself, which came on the third and fourth days of the convention, all in an atmosphere not exactly conducive to thoughtful deliberative action.

Finally, to see the setting fully, David J. McDonald was differently situated from most union presidents. His best friends conceded that "McDonald had a most difficult time taking over from Murray. Nobody has ever forgotten Murray, he was a dedicated man."

*   *   *   *

The steelworkers felt deep gratitude to Philip Murray, whose leadership had lifted them from the lower depths; he was the pioneer-organizer and builder of their union. There was a feeling of kinship too; although he had been a miner, not a steelworker, he was one of their own, and he had never lost contact with them. They were aware, of course, that Murray in the later years lived in Washington, met with the great and the powerful, up to and including the President and his Cabinet officers. They assumed that he had to do those things as their representative, but that on his own he felt most at home in their neighborhood, among them.

Philip Murray was the unchallenged leader of the USWA. The union was his creation, inasmuch as this can be said of any one man in the development of a mass organization of over a million and a quarter members. Only the Communists had ever attempted to challenge Murray's power, and had made no headway. Murray was not too democratic. Some even said he thought he was doing the Lord's work. He himself probably never entertained the notion, but other people did. Murray's word was the readily accepted law of the USWA.

But the man who took over after Murray's sudden death in 1952 left it to the Lord to attend to His work and proceeded to his own task. There was much to be done. McDonald had rapidly entered the vacuum of power left by Murray's death without too much advice and consent. There were misgivings.

Although McDonald had been secretary-treasurer of the steelworkers' organization from the start, he had never been either a miner or a steelworker. Moreover, he did not seem to have "the touch"; he was a man apart in 1956. The steelworkers had been ready "to take most anything from Phil," but Mr. McDonald was to be judged by performance. He had to build a mass feeling for himself and in this he never quite succeeded. His radio and TV programs made him known but not loved. When dissatisfaction developed in 1956, he made many attempts to restore the badly shattered unity, at least among the union's intermediate layers. District conferences were held in disturbed areas. Staffers were mobilized to "make friends and influence people." The show at the 1958 convention was calculated to implement that program. In the end none of it helped.

Some convention watchers suggested that the violent attack on the obviously feeble Rarick-led "opposition" was staged so as to project the threat of an enemy within the ranks to bolster fading loyalties and cement greater membership cohesion. Their thought was that since automatic unionism, continuous improvement in work terms, and dues-checkoff had tended to reduce the members' contact and concern with the union, a homemade enemy had to be created. Another theory was that, having removed the Communists and no longer having an enemy within, various union groups had begun fighting among themselves.

Such suppositions might have fitted other union situations, particularly where the democratic process was on permanent furlough. But the steelworkers did not need a synthetic opposition. To them democracy, for all its shortcomings, is for real. They are a tough-minded lot. Their 1958 convention was plainly sitting in judgment on a group of men who 18 months earlier had challenged the very administration which, by and large, had "made the revolution." For its part that administration chose to overlook the fact that the revolution of the 1930s and '40s was made by all, and that disagreements among winning revolutionists who then become "the government" are a legitimate fair price to pay for victory and democracy.

Flogging a Dead Horse

Having determined on a showdown, McDonald wasted no time and minced no words. Invoking the revered name of Philip Murray, his opening address called for war to the death on the opposition:

> Standing on this very spot . . . in his last speech in this Convention Hall, the great Phil Murray said: "Your union cannot be destroyed by the enemies from within." And I pledge to you, Phil Murray, and I pledge to you delegates, and I pledge to the 1,250,000 members of the USWA, that I will not permit the enemies from within to destroy this union of yours.

The call to arms was answered by a standing ovation. Delegates paraded to the rostrum with banners and posters bearing slogans thoughtfully prepared in advance. The union president then warned the delegates what to expect from the opposition:

They are going to try to make this convention a shambles
. . . to stir up racial antagonism . . . they will use every
iniquitous force that they can command here—the Communists, the Trotskyites, the NAM agents, the company
agents that are wandering around this city. . . . They are
going to fall back on the old Communist party line which
I have heard expressed in the year 1924 in the United Mineworkers convention—the old Communist line that the staff
representatives must be elected.

McDonald then went on to accuse the opposition leaders of
personal dishonesty:

They have no program of a constructive nature. They
have only a program of hate . . . of greed . . . two top
leaders of this group have now filed in the Court of Common Pleas . . . individual lawsuits totaling one million
dollars and addressed at McDonald . . . Greed! They
want to dig it out of your pockets . . . out of your treasury for their own personal use. And that is what their
lawsuits say—$1 million.

Referring to magazine articles that had described his weaknesses as a leader and had forecast his eventual ouster from
office, McDonald told the convention:

The personal attacks . . . I can take. . . . These vicious
outpourings are not primarily directed against McDonald.
They are directed against . . . the United Steelworkers of
America, and I am merely the symbol which they would
destroy.

* * *

And I say to you . . . if you want your union to be clean
and strong don't leave it to the Great White Father, as
I am now being called in the south, to do it. Rip this
cancer out of your bowels through your own doing . . .
Rise up, you Strong Men of Steel. . . . Show those who

hate you and show . . . all the people of the world the
real tough metal of which you are made.

McDonald was again given "a long standing ovation," the
opposition leaders were booed and their expulsion from the union
demanded. Those in opposition watched the performance quietly.
They made no attempt to interrupt the demonstrators, for they
numbered less than 100 persons and clearly were unable "to make
the convention a shambles," as McDonald charged.

The union president's course was unorthodox. Not that the
flamboyant oratory was unusual. Formal union presidential pres-
entations usually are high-pitched. (Only John L. Lewis could
be murderously effective without raising his voice.) Philip Murray
had moved hearts, caused rising anger in audiences while talking
quietly, slowly, as if he were thinking on his feet, but not many
can do that. What was unusual in McDonald's performance was
his use of the opening address to attack an unimportant, politically
inconsequential opposition. The keynote convention speech customarily spells out broad union objectives. "Shop talk" is usually
left for a later session. By opening the convention with an attack
on the opposition, McDonald gave the dissidents an importance
that in fact they lacked. He clearly wanted to set the scene for
a political lynching, and in this he succeeded.

True, the union president did not confine himself to the
enemy within. He also referred to the steel industry's growing
hostility toward the union. He spoke bitterly against the employers who had rejected the doctrine of mutual trusteeship which
McDonald had been urging on them as "a doctrine which was
thoroughly American in concept." The delegates heartily ap-
plauded when, warning the industry, he said:

Well, I prefer peace. I have tried to teach the doctrine of
mutual trusteeship, and I still believe it is sound. I prefer
peace through collective bargaining, but if the steel industry wants a long strike, I guarantee them that the
United Steelworkers will give it to them.

But the delegates' reaction to the attack on the employers was not nearly as vigorous as their response to McDonald's assaults on the "cancer in their bowels"—the dissidents within, which really touched an exposed nerve.

McDonald was not without support on this point. He was the spokesman for nearly all in the assembly. Not the lone-wolf type of leader, he willingly worked with the group. Moreover, as he told the convention, he liked the power and glory of office:

> Mine is a great job. People say I am proud and believe me, I am proud . . . to be the President of the United Steelworkers of America. Who wouldn't be proud to have this great privilege of representing you, not only as a chairman of a convention, but . . . in collective bargaining conferences . . . in the councils of the AFL-CIO . . . in the field of foreign affairs . . . in the councils of government . . . all over the world, speaking your philosophy. Of course I am proud, and anybody who would stand up on this platform . . . and say he isn't proud of these things would be a fool.

But the McDonald speech, or battle cry, evoked from outsiders the anticipated response—"flogging a dead horse." Why was it necessary?

The administration could not possibly have feared a Second Coming by Donald C. Rarick and his colleagues. The circumstances that had made them the wonder of labor in 1957 no longer existed. The "dues protest" movement was dead, Rarick was politically finished, as all the delegates knew even if Rarick did not.

Arthur J. Goldberg, then USWA General Counsel and valued adviser, had strongly urged the administration against the course it pursued. His advice was not taken because the delegates had been persuaded by the district leaders that a powerful demonstration of unity and an impressive humiliation of the handful of remaining oppositionists would improve the union's position in the forthcoming contract renewal negotiations with the steel corporations. Once aroused, and their sense of union loyalty inflamed, crowd psychology took over. Thus a great union, democratic in its very nature and in the beliefs of great numbers of its members, turned into a frenzied mob engaged in a disturbingly nondemocratic performance.

In an effort to survive, the Rarick group then advanced some proposals to "democratize" the union, but exhibited no great wisdom either in its choice of proposed reforms or in the quality of debate on them.

The major issue with which the Rarick people launched their renewed battle was the proposed amendment under which field representatives or agents would be elected by the local unions instead of being appointed by the General Office. This issue might have caused excitement in the old days, when a two-year term for union officers, referendum elections, and recall of officers were considered the heart of progressivism. But union views of how a union should be run had greatly changed. Unionists had come to consider such problems pragmatically, and they now felt that one method of setting up the administrative apparatus might work well in one instance and not in another. In some cases a combination of methods might seem practicable. Actual practice at the time of the convention, as ever since, was not based on any fixed theory of union government, but on specific union needs and developments. At times, of course, a change in the prevailing custom may be induced by considerations of power politics. It is conceivable that in other circumstances a majority of the USWA delegates who bitterly rejected the opposition motion for electing the staffers might have enthusiastically supported it (with the exception of those directly and professionally tied to the administration). The Rarick group had banked on the clear demagogical appeal of the proposal. It might have worked if the opposition and administration had been more evenly matched.

Debate on the issue was unruly, violent, and marked by boos, heckling, interruptions. Eventually McDonald secured silence and order prevailed, with the hatred in the eyes of the combatants speaking louder than the previous shouts. But even when uninterrupted the opposition arguments fell on tight-closed ears.

For the administration which earlier had created the climate in which passion ruled supreme, in a spirit of true democratic parliamentarianism, finally did give the opposition a hearing—an opportunity to speak to the full extent of its spokesmens' lung power. Indeed the standard rule limiting speakers "from the floor" to five minutes was suspended by a nearly unanimous vote of the delegates.

McDonald saw to it that every member of the opposition who so desired was given an opportunity to speak. Rarick, leader of the reform proponents and central target of the majority, was repeatedly accorded the courtesy and convenience of speaking from the rostrum, although the steelworkers' president clearly wished him no political glory. Opposition supporters were given enough rope, which was just about all they gained. When the vote was called, only 50 of the over 3,500 delegates stood up for the reform motion.

The opposition then promptly proposed, with the support of only six local unions, another reform. This motion called for a change in Provisions G and H of Article XII, Section I, in the union constitution. Provision G prohibits "slandering or wilfully wronging a member of the International Union." Provision H prohibits "using abusive language or disturbing the peace and harmony of any meeting in or around any office or meeting place of the International Union." The opposition argued that these provisions were foreign and hostile to union democracy and union ideals. They proposed that Paragraph G be expunged and Paragraph H be amended to prohibit only "using violent methods to disturb or disrupt a meeting of a local union or of the International Union."

On the face of it, what the opposition appeared to want was freedom from restrictions on resorting to "slander or wilful wrongdoing against a member" and also to legitimatize the use of "abusive language" or any other means short of "violent methods" to "disturb or to disrupt the peace at or around any meeting of the union."

The proponents of the constitutional amendments may have meant well. Administrative genius at times indeed uses these restrictive injunctions to stifle and curb dissenters on the pretext that they "disrupt peace and harmony." Nonetheless it is difficult to imagine a sillier way of coping with the evil than that proposed by the Rarick group. In effect they asked for the right to "do wrong" to union members in order to protect union democracy and "union high ideals."

Only two delegates spoke on the proposed amendments, rather feebly arguing that the clause in the constitution that prohibits slander was being used by "the tyrants against honest criticism." The motion went down to overwhelming defeat. Only 24 of the 3550 delegates voted in favor, about half of the dismal support rallied by the Rarick group for its previous motion.

The contest between an all-powerful administration in control of 98 percent of the convention and the small, disjointed, and incompetent opposition came to its predestined end with the introduction of a Special Resolution by the Convention Committee on Resolutions. Couched in the high-flown verbiage of democratic principle, the resolution was punitive in the extreme. It called on the local unions and, as a court of last resort, on the International Executive Board to put the opposition leaders on trial with a view to their expulsion from the union. Joseph Molony, top-ranking union officer and the Secretary of the Resolutions Committee, closed his argument for the purge operation with these words:

> This is an emotional situation, [but] in this resolution you have the great tradition of our union. There is no lynch law in the United Steelworkers of America. These people will be given a fair trial and if found guilty will be delivered from our midst.
>
>   *   *   *
>
> To Messers Rarick and Mamula and O'Brien, in advance of charges being filed, in advance of the findings of their local unions and the International Executive Board, and solely because of their conduct at this Convention, I say to these bitter men: depart from our halls. There is no place for you in the United Steelworkers of America.

The power play ended with an avalanche of votes in favor of the resolution. Only two delegates registered dissent. The convention roared its satisfaction. Justice had been done. The union was saved from a danger that was neither clear nor present, which in no real sense existed.

Judged by their conduct in 1958 and two years later at the 1960 convention, Rarick and his associate leaders posed no threat to the USWA; instead, they were their own worst enemies. The only charge that would have stood up against them in a court of justice was that of attempting political suicide.

Curiously enough, insurgent leader Rarick made a positive personal impression. A healthy, vigorous, muscular man, he was the kind that generally appeals to labor audiences. But his presentation lacked force. He was anything but skillful in marshaling arguments, and at times he seemed incapable of doing so. Perhaps he had assembled his notes in logical order before ascending the rostrum; but though he consulted them frequently, he could give only a disjointed speech. McDonald, in contrast, spoke with force and authority as head of the union. He was accustomed to platform performance and was in complete control of the situation. Perhaps Rarick might have done better if he had had a vital issue but he had none. In addition, Nick Mamula, a bit more skilled on the platform, was not a first-rate speaker or leader. Frank O'Brien was similarly poorly equipped to help win a union power coup.

Thus weak in leadership, the opposition in the 1958 convention was a fragmented force with no clinching issue, divided in fact even on the old dues protest and its subsequent "reform" measures. Mr. O'Brien, for example, told the delegates that, on the dues question, he would now split the difference between the old $3 monthly assessment and the new $5 assessment, making the dues $4 a month. For his part, Mr. Rarick announced that he would abide by a majority decision.

Rarick was not a quitter, but unfortunately he was not too discriminating in his choice of weapons. In 1957 Rarick broke a basic union law by taking his case to court before exhausting internal means for seeking redress of grievances. Although he might have argued that his chances of securing justice in the union in the circumstances were like those of a snowball in hell, nonetheless he had violated union law. Again in 1958 he committed another grave tactical blunder. Angered by his defeat in the convention, Rarick returned to his home state of Pennsylvania and threw himself into local politics, supporting the political campaign of Republican party candidate Arthur T. McGonigle against the Democrats' David Lawrence, who had the support of organized labor. In so doing he not only further antagonized union leaders and members but also his own followers, who refused to join him in this political venture.

Despite his defeat at the 1958 convention, Rarick, apparently convinced that he had picked the right issue in '58 by substituting union democracy for the once-successful issue of keeping dues low, re-formed his opposition into an Organization for Members' Rights. His OMR group met with even worse luck in the 1960 convention than had the old opposition in 1958. The OMR secured only a dozen votes on a test issue.

As reported in the *Monthly Labor Review*,[1] "The atmosphere [in the 1960 convention] was marked by name calling and issuance of charges and countercharges. Scuffles occurred both on and off the convention floor, one of which involved Rarick personally. President McDonald appointed a committee to investigate circumstances surrounding this fight following Rarick's telegram to Secretary of Labor James P. Mitchell asking him to 'bring full protection of the law . . . to safeguard the rank-and-file members of the United Steelworkers.'"

In a reply letter, Rarick was informed that the Justice Department would investigate whether there were violations of the criminal provisions of the 1959 Labor Act (the LMRDA, now generally known as the Landrum-Griffin Act).

Continuing the fight, Rarick's OMR announced a slate of candidates for the referendum election in February 1961, with Rarick for USWA president and Joseph W. Murray, son of the late leader Philip Murray, for vice-president. No candidate was listed for secretary-treasurer, thereby giving tacit endorsement to the incumbent I. W. Abel, long a commanding member of the McDonald team, and the man who four years later wrested the presidency from McDonald. Abel promptly rejected Rarick's support, and Joseph Murray announced that he was no candidate for any office. Late in December, the union announced that Rarick had failed to obtain the required number of nominations

(40 were needed) to appear on the election ballots. So far as his ambitions in 1962 were concerned, he was finished. He could hardly look forward with hope to the next elections in 1965.

In his closing remarks adjourning the 1958 convention, McDonald expressed regret that so much time had been taken up with "the so-called Dues Protest Committee." And he added,

> . . . you can see, all of you, that this problem of the Dues Protest Committee was certainly magnified out of all proportion to its true importance. You will recall that on the special resolution affecting those members of our Union, only two votes were cast against its adoption.

And deploring that some very important matters had not received the attention they merited, McDonald said:

> I tried to be democratic. I have always been democratic in the conduct of our Conventions.

*   *   *   *

> All allegations to the contrary notwithstanding, everybody had his say, even more than his say on this subject, and despite anything which they may attempt to have published, even they cannot deny this fact.

It was true. The opposition had had its say, just as a convicted man has his "last statement" before being sentenced. But in this instance there had been a conviction without a trial.

Union "Crime and Punishment"

A fair-minded judge investigating the USWA 1958 convention would probably render a "Scotch verdict": not guilty but don't do it again. No hosannas were due. On the other hand, no written law of union democracy had been openly violated; an honest judge—or observer—could only wring his hands.

Rarick had dared to seek the highest union office and had almost gotten away with it. That in itself was sinful, of course, especially for a man who was merely one of 3000 local union presidents in the USWA and had no national standing. But his overambition was after all not a statutory crime and his defeat was in a way a claim to forgiveness. What could not be forgiven was his refusal to accept defeat.

Loyalty to the organization is a basic obligation of all unionists who take themselves and their union seriously. The leader is to be followed once he is generally accepted. This point was expressed by Joseph Molony, secretary of the Committee on Resolutions, who introduced the Special Resolution indicting the opposition leaders. Mr. Molony some years earlier had sought the vice-presidency of the union in opposition to Howard Hague, the McDonald candidate. Molony even then had an impressive record in the USWA, and his candidacy was considered a challenge to McDonald. Referring to that election in his remarks at the 1958 Convention, Molony said in part:

> I don't want to flog a dead horse, but reference has been made to the so-called Molony campaign. To hear Mr. Rarick talk, you would think that no one else in this union has ever raised himself up and exerted himself and used his constitutional rights. Hell, we had rebels in this union before Rarick was a member.

*   *   *   *

> It is true that at one time I sought high office in this union. I am proud that I had the opportunity.

*   *   *   *

> I was beaten by Howard Hague, and I recognize Howard Hague as the Vice-President of the United Steelworkers.

To this very moment Delegate Rarick does not recognize President McDonald as our President.

* * * *

When I and the good people who supported me were beaten—and beaten fairly and squarely—I didn't sue my beloved union for a million dollars, and I didn't attack the character and integrity of my friend, Dave McDonald.

It is unlikely that Molony no longer thought himself better qualified for the office of vice-president than incumbent Howard Hague; nor, for that matter, less capable to lead the union than McDonald himself. But that was his secret. In public he was guided by the prevailing position of union officers, a variation on the basic theme of union solidarity on the membership level: all for one and one for all.

The fight against Rarick was more than a mopping up operation; it was also a preventive war to discourage any future, better-equipped Rarick from appearing out of the nowhere and trying to get places, perhaps actually getting to *the* place. That would not have been the case if Abel, Hague, Molony, or Whitehouse had moved at the time for McDonald's high post. And indeed when such a move was in fact made several years later, it was quite another chess game. Abel, Hague, Molony and the other district directors, as members of the International Executive Board, together wielded controlling power in the union. They naturally supported McDonald and the administration, that is themselves. Just as they generously praised McDonald, they condemned Rarick with full-lunged voices. "Throw the stinking stooges . . . out on their ears," district director Al Whitehouse demanded, "and close our ranks and stand solidly and completely 1,000 percent behind our beloved, our great, our dynamic leader."

Other high-ranking members of the administration similarly spoke out, each doing his duty to the best of his ability. In defending the union president these men were indeed fulfilling an obligation of office. As custodians of power, they were well aware of the importance of the orderly transfer of power. Thus, if Dave should ever become unable to hold on to the presidency (as happened a few years later), it would be in the best interest of the union that the succession be determined not casually or by accident, but by a careful process of selection. The members had a right to vote for a candidate competently selected by responsible men. And who were the responsible men if not the district directors? It was their duty to think ahead. That was why Rarick's defeat and humiliation had to be complete.

The operation was not technically in conflict with democracy. Succession is a serious matter and concern with it is not necessarily contrary to the democratic process, provided that it does not undermine individual rights, which are both the basis and purpose of democracy. The indicting resolution presented by Mr. Molony and adopted by the convention stressed the union's commitment to democracy, including the members' rights to dissent from and to criticize union policies and officers. One "but," however, was strongly underscored:

> We take no exception to those who openly and through the regular procedures established under our constitution, have voiced their views and their opposition to the organization's officers and policies, however misguided such opposition may be. But we do take strong exception to the ringleaders who, outside our channels, have taken actions designed to serve the interests of the enemies of our union and of organized labor, and who otherwise have committed flagrant violations of our constitution.

Rarick's right to run for high office was not questioned. The resolution made it clear that his crime consisted in violating union rules by turning to the courts for vindication, thereby "serving the interests of the union's enemies." And under the rules, the union convention was the proper authority to review his conduct, judge it, and if need be, recommend punitive action. All this was in line with the rules; yet it would be difficult to find a less appropriate setting for a judicious determination than a convention of thousands of delegates who have been worked up to a frenzy by inflammatory oratory and who proceed to boo and shout derisively while the dissenters are "having their say."

Democracy is prettier in books than in life, being operated not by angels but people. Since the struggle for influence and mastery is of the essence in the democratic process, individuals and groups accordingly line up against one another to seek a hearing and victory for their respective ideas and objectives. When head-on encounters occur in the political state, there is a real measure of protection for both the body politic and individuals in such institutional devices as functioning political parties, a free press, an independent judiciary, and other democratic safeguards spelled out in the Constitution and Bill of Rights. But the unions have no similar devices to protect their internal democracy. Political parties are not tolerated in unions and would make little sense under the governing concept of unionism that the common and overriding interest of all workers is in their dealings with the employers. This in no way relates to the Marxian concept of a social-class interest but derives from a unity of interest in collective bargaining. Unions recognize the right of members to have differences of opinion about how a union is to be operated and who is to have authority, but they do not effectively protect dissenters.

Early unionism evolved arrangements and provisions, really no more than gentlemen's agreements, which served to keep internal conflicts within bounds and essential unity undamaged; the moral weight of the union's constitution and special bylaws sufficed to secure compliance. The local union, the national union convention, in some instances referendum voting on important decisions, and election of national officers by referendum were the key supports of internal democracy, as they still are.

The concept of unity as the core of union, embracing the basic interests of all members, precluded the need for separating legislative, administrative, and judicial powers. Any such separation of powers would have seemed an absurdity to the first unions struggling for a toehold in the nation's economy. Their members never dreamed that as a result of the growth of unions into huge and complex organizations, their toehold would one day become two feet solidly planted on economic ground; that, in fact, as part of the national economy, unions would need to develop concomitant responsibilities. These responsibilities would go beyond those immediately pertaining to union; union would become so big as to constitute not only a world of its own, but a world that is a part of the social fabric of the nation.

All this has happened. But most unions have been lamentably slow in adapting to the new realities. Meanwhile, as members develop differing views, the need for fair, objective machinery for resolving disputes becomes ever more urgent. This is a central need.

The Steelworkers Convention described in these pages abided by all of its constitutional provisions. "Trouble" in this convention was due not to any violation of democracy, but in the way the judicial process functioned.

The right to govern by mandate of majority decision does not automatically exclude intelligent consideration of minority opposition. Very possibly Msgr. George Higgins was reminding the convention of this fact when, the day after its unseemly performance of *Crime and Punishment*, he closed the final session with this prayer:

> . . . Help us to resist the inevitable temptation to exaggerate the virtues of our friends and the faults of our opponents. Give us the grace to temper our laudable zeal for the cause of organized labor with a saving sense of balance and perspective, with a sense of humor based on the virtues of humility and fraternal charity.

Father Higgins' prayer was in effect a suggestion that the time has come for unions to be governed by "a sense of balance and perspective" in their internal relations, even as they are so governed in industrial relations.

Shortly after the turbulent convention was adjourned, second thoughts began to disturb the victors. The whole affair began to look rather silly when the three insurgents, so severely indicted at Atlantic City, were tried by their respective local unions as requested by the convention, and were cleared and returned to their command posts as local union presidents. Vindication of the oppositionists did not necessarily prove that local members shared their views. Local unions sometimes make a show of independence from the national higher-ups in small matters, but tend to fall in line when vital issues are at stake. In the circumstances, the International Executive Board decided to shelve the case of the three renegades, since, as they now saw it, Rarick was of no immediate consequence and, given time, would by his own foolishness undo the little that may have remained of his once-upon-a-time prestige. The calculation proved correct.

Meanwhile labor-management relations grew tense. The 116-day steel strike was in the offing. And soon enough a former dues protester was quoted as saying: "The strike has united us as never before." It united the steel companies too. Roger M. Blough, Chairman of the Board of the U.S. Steel Corporation, spearheaded the move "to put the union in its place." He said the union had become "a force which well surpasses the strength of any group of private organizations this country has ever known . . . a force no one company or even one industry could begin to equal." As leader of the entire basic steel industry, which he had corralled to fight the union, he asked whether it was not ". . . time to raise the question of whether the original purpose so many sincere people had in fostering the cause of unions has somehow gotten out of hand? Should we ask whether nationwide wage policies, industry-wide strike power, the ability to shut down whole industries and to bring economic America to its knees is necessary or right?" [2]

The moral question raised by the wrong man at the wrong time was answered by the reality of the strike and in subsequent encounters. U. S. Steel and the other steel companies are still in business and yearly report record profits. Labor held its own. Later an irate President, John F. Kennedy, himself nurtured in wealth, exploded not against the unions but against the steel magnates and businessmen in general, citing the judgment of his father, Joseph Kennedy, that they were "all sons of bitches."

Life has its own jests, often illuminating more than any book the meaning of events. Thus there was an ironic postscript to the occurrences at the USWA convention described in this chapter when I. W. Abel challenged McDonald's power and became president of the USWA on June 1, 1965. As head of the nation's third-largest union (only the Auto Workers and the Teamsters have larger constituencies) and an intelligent, hard-working person, he has since become one of the nation's most important labor leaders. Abel's victory was won by a 10,000-vote margin (out of 610,000 votes) over McDonald, who had lost the leadership long before the voting began.

Labor analyst John Herling, author of *Right to Challenge*, the definitive book on the steelworkers, commented at the time, "If Mr. Abel had not been assured he had the majority of the Executive Board, he would not have attempted to run in the first place." [3]

Abel is an intensely skilled, experienced labor man, and an astute politician. Nevertheless, the vote with which he ousted McDonald was substantially less than that of his running mates. On the same slate with him, Walter Burke won the post of secretary-treasurer by 45,000 votes. Joseph Molony came in as vice-president by a 22,000 vote margin over the McDonald candidate. By conforming to union mores after his first bid for the office failed, Molony made it on this second try.

At first McDonald threatened to file election complaints under the LMRDA. But in the end he announced that, "for the good of the union," he would not press charges. The gesture was sincerely appreciated.

As Herling's *Labor Letter* pointed out, McDonald's free spending, flashy ways, including an $1800-a-month hotel suite in Washington and a second home in Palm Springs, did not sit well with the members or district directors, one of whom Herling quoted as having said at the time, "Union discontent grew with having an absentee overlord as president."

Nonetheless, as everyone knows, union presidents are not easily removed from office. Abel obviously has the leadership qualities that McDonald lacked. Yet with all his demonstrated capacities, and they are many, Abel could not have come to power unless the McDonald hold on power had already been loosened. It had indeed been weakened by McDonald's overreliance on outside experts, his alienation from the membership and middle-echelon leadership, his failure to cement the layers, from base to peak, of that pyramid of union power on which the authority of every labor leader rests. The hollowness of his command had been clearly demonstrated by that hero-victim Rarick, who so many years before, with his startling feat of getting 223,516 votes in a bid for the presidency, had revealed for all to see the shakiness of McDonald's hold on office.

The fact that Abel bided his time, laboring for seven years before making his successful bid for command, indicates how thorough, patient, and careful a strategist he is. Additionally Abel has since, in the office of president, shown that he has an innovative, constructive approach to labor problems within a societal framework. The steelworkers also have in him an excellent negotiator. The change was for the good.

Depending on the viewpoint, it can be said that the same democratic processes that defeated and humiliated Rarick, and in turn McDonald, worked for and elevated Abel; or it can be said that the whole sequence was an undemocratic power play. Another conclusion, and one which perhaps comes closer to reality, may be that democracy works best for those who best understand the deep, contradictory, and vast scope of forces involved in its operation, not excluding the subtle and intimate relations of leaders and the led. No one can hope to win in politics who does not have political sense. Union politics are as fiercely competitive, if not more so, than politics anywhere else. Internal union democracy was strengthened, despite some of the ugly episodes explored in these pages, episodes that in a way were a journey through Purgatory, not to Paradise, but toward the kind of decent, down-to-earth democracy which by and large prevails in the USWA.

7

LEADERS AND THE LED

The exploration of several specific labor situations in the last two chapters suggests the continuing validity of an old truth, that theories alone cannot explain basic social conflicts but must be blended with workaday realities.

Justice Oliver Wendell Holmes once said, "The life of the law has not been logic, it has been experience." So too is experience the life of labor. Holmes pointed out that in any attempt to codify laws "into a series of seemingly self-sufficient propositions, those propositions will be but a phase in a continuous growth." And he noted that we must know the past in order to gain knowledge of the present. In Holmes's view, "The law is always approaching and never reaching consistency. It is forever adopting new principles from life at one end, and it always retains old ones from history at the other, which have not yet been absorbed or sloughed off. It will become entirely consistent only when it ceases to grow."

Labor, too, is an evolving entity, as inconsistent as the living law. The active men in the union movement endow their work with a commitment to values which they perceive as inviolate. Their views of human relations and their concepts of justice admittedly are not as coolly dispassionate as those of scholars. Participation makes for a certain difference. The same battle looks and is different to those who are in it and to those who watch through field glasses from a distance. In the labor movement, as in all experience, detail is important. That is why Chapters 2 through 6 were devoted to what seemed to be significant detail to this observer participant.

If labor leaders were readers they would recognize the abiding truth in another of Holmes's statements: "It is required of a man that he must share the action and passion of his time at peril of being judged never to have lived."

The solely job-oriented member or the leader who views himself as primarily a merchandiser of labor may each assign different meanings to "having lived." Together, both are likely to differ from members and leaders who take the broad inclusive view of the union enterprise and who therefore truly "share the action and passion" of our time. In the long run, the difference matters little. The over-all dynamic of the union movement spurs on the willing and understanding unionists and drags along the uncomprehending and reluctant toward the same complex end. That end is organization for power, mobilization of power for an ever-expanding multiplicity and diversity of function and participation in the life and contests of the nation. The dynamic of American unionism is of the bone and flesh of the dynamic of America—the unwillingness to stay put, an irresistible urge to get going, move on, reach out.

This is not to be overgeneralized. Woodrow Wilson's statement about public officeholders applies to men in union office: "Some grow, some grow fat." Union democracy, if intelligently practiced, may contribute toward growth without danger of obesity.

In the discussion of internal union democracy in Chapter 3, five fundamental questions were formulated (page 62). They were based on the premise that the problems of making democracy work within the unions can be dealt with adequately only within the context of experience. The report of actuality situations in Chapters 4, 5 and 6 were, in effect, the raw materials of the search for answers.

The first query asked whether the unionist rank-and-file by its own momentum can maintain a democratic government, resisting usurpation of power by its leaders.

In the case of the International Longshoreman's Association, the decent union set up by the AFL failed to gain the vote necessary to dislodge the gangster crew in power. But in the struggle for control in circumstances of terror, a good half of the longshoremen staked their jobs and risked their lives to vote for a decent union. They lost because the reformers did not deliver on initial promises. It was a case, and not the only one, in which the courage and good sense of the membership was way ahead of the leadership.

In another case, not explored in these pages but meriting mention, the corrupt Bakery and Confectionery Workers' International Union ruled by Jimmy Cross was expelled from the Federation. The AFL-CIO subsequently launched the decent new American Bakery and Confectionery Workers, which in time put the corrupt old union out of business. In this instance leadership delivered and was equal in courage to the membership. But it should be noted that the terror in the bakeries, while real, was not comparable to the terror on the waterfront, nor was the underworld involved.

In the United Brotherhood of Carpenters and Joiners other circumstances militated against the efforts of the few who wanted to replace machine dominance with democratic procedures at national headquarters. Knowledgeable persons assert that the carpenters have a substantial measure of freedom on the local level. The question arises, however, whether freedom measured is freedom in fact. Obviously it is not. But the top outfit of the "empire in wood" has exerted unbreakable control for more than half a century, ever since the days of William Hutcheson, the original empire builder; his son has since ruled with the same autocratic hand and local men no longer think they can do anything about it. They have stopped trying. This does not mean that a new situation in the industry or a break in the dynasty may not provide a sudden opportunity for democracy to move in; there are enough dissatisfied elements in the membership to be on the alert for such an opportunity.

The instance of the Steelworkers union was entirely different from that of the UBCJ, for what was involved in the USWA was not basic democratic principle, but the modes of applying that principle; and in that, the rank-and-file in no way differed from the leaders. The USWA was and is a democratic union; but in it, as elsewhere, sometimes democracy gets the short end of the stick.

As indicated in the case histories discussed earlier, there are two main handicaps to the progress of internal union democracy;

lack of an unbiased, independent and authoritative judicial process and of a genuinely free labor press. These deficiencies obtain nearly everywhere in the labor movement. The honorable exceptions only emphasize the unsatisfactory generality. It is fair to note, however, that by and large rank-and-file union members can be depended on to support democratic versus autocratic "clique" government, when and where the odds against them are not overwhelming. In the unions as elsewhere, democracy is not a one-man or one-group operation. If public aid can be given to help promote democracy in developing areas abroad, perhaps the home front, represented by labor, should not be entirely neglected. Whether labor would welcome such public assistance is, of course, dubious. That the need exists is clear.

The second question asked in Chapter 3 was: How well equipped are the unions to deal with the problems of ethics and democracy in the evolving new circumstances of labor activity and outlook?

As shown by the examples already cited, the unhappy answer is that most unions lack effective structural devices—binding laws and procedural practices—to establish and maintain the kind of ethics that promote democracy and the kind of democracy that supports ethical standards in a mutual two-way flow. Professor Joel Seidman of the University of Chicago, author of *Union Rights and Union Duties*, and of a number of other valuable labor studies, at one time examined the constitutions of ninety-three national unions. His conclusions are very pertinent to this discussion and are therefore, with the author's permission, quoted here in the following excerpts: [1]

[It] is a rare union that recognizes, in its basic legal document, the right of an opposition group to form, to raise the necessary funds, and to reach the membership with its program of action. The official journal functions in most cases as the mouthpiece of the administration, rather than as a medium for discussion of the merits of opposing political programs or tendencies within the union.

*   *   *

Union constitutions are studded with clauses forbidding false accusations or misrepresentations, conduct detrimental to the best interests of the union or unbecoming a member, statements reflecting upon the character or questioning the integrity of an officer, and actions tending to disrupt the union or to bring it into disrepute. In many unions it would be difficult to conduct an effective political campaign without running the risk of charges for violating clauses such as the above.

* * *

In most unions the incumbents would play an important part in the judicial process, helping to determine whether their political opponents had violated vague language of the type quoted above.

* * *

It is hard to read union constitutions without being struck by the many provisions dealing with the obligations and the disciplining of members, as against the relatively small number of sections concerned with members' rights within the organization.

Summed up, Dr. Siedman's findings are:

Only two union constitutions have clauses which allow factional political groups to operate inside the unions, the International Typographical Union and the International Ladies Garment Workers Union.

The constitutions of seven unions contain clauses barring "dual union" activities of members, but the clauses are so worded that they could apply to a member involved in a factional fight with the union officers. Eight more unions have "dual union" provisions which appear to make impossible the functioning of opposition groups.

In 76 other unions, the "dual union" clause is so vague that it could be used against "internal political groups," or else there is a broad disciplinary provision that can be used against opponents of the officers.

Only eight unions guarantee that candidates for office

can obtain space for statements in the official union papers, or guarantee that members can express their views on internal politics in the papers.

Only two unions have impartial review boards to hear complaints of members against their officers and to overrule the officers' actions.

Dr. Seidman doubts whether the LMRDA is equipped to meet the task of filling existing gaps in the internal union democratic performance. Agreeing with Dr. Clark Kerr that "the labor movement is well established now, in legal protection as well as in the support of its members," Dr. Seidman proposes, in effect, the same cure suggested by Dr. Kerr for the internal union malady:

. . . recognize internal opposition to the administration group as legitimate rather than as subversive, guarantee groups of members the right to organize politically and reach the membership with their programs, and revamp disciplinary procedures to give assurance that vague phrases will not be used by incumbents to punish those whose real offense is political opposition.

To organize politically is not a clear term, but if it means only the right of the members to communicate with one another, why should that be made contingent on the unions "now being well established"? There never has been any valid reason for denying members the right to communicate with each other about their ideas and programs for running their unions. This is quite different from creating permanent political parties in the unions, which, for reasons cited earlier, seems to this writer to be a self-defeating proposal.

As to the third central question in Chapter 3, which raised the issue of whether democracy and efficiency in union government are at all compatible, and whether democratic operation is even possible in big unions dealing with big industry and big government, all the evidence indicates that the assumed conflict between democracy and efficiency is neither real nor relevant. Nor is there any inherent necessity for bigness to diminish internal democracy. The need is for evolving new procedures for making internal democracy function within a newly enlarged and enlarging context. It is true that some leaders tend to brush democratic procedures aside as being cumbersome and inefficient. That does not make them so. And it is true that when those responsible for the operation of democratic processes fail to make them work properly, the tendency is to blame "bigness," or an alleged conflict with efficiency, for the failure. Similarly, this tendency in no wise establishes guilt. Sometimes the culprit must be sought elsewhere. Actual experience in this area is inconclusive. Some examples of how the problem presents itself in a few outstanding unions follow:

The United Mineworkers of America under John L. Lewis was a very efficiently run union—or seemed to be—and it was run from the national center by John L. Lewis as undemocratically as a union can be run. It is true that the miners' locals were free to manage their internal affairs, and no objection was made to their passing various resolutions on national union affairs, which were invariably bypassed by the national conventions. John L. Lewis was, of course, enormously powerful from the mid-1930s on through all the decades in which he ruled the UMWA. For good and ill, there has never been another like him on the labor scene.

The International Ladies Garment Workers Union and the International Association of Machinists are among the most efficiently run unions in the nation; yet the local unions and lodges function democratically without any impairment of the unions' effectiveness. As to the centers of authority in these unions, as in most unions, accommodation is the governing principle.

The giant United Automobile Workers of America is outstanding for its efficiency and democracy. Here neither bigness nor effective smooth operation seems to present any insoluble problems in the maintenance of a thoroughly democratic organization. Its Public Review Board, which has no parallel in any of the other big unions, is, as previously noted, one of the central girders of democracy in the UAW.

The United Steelworkers of America is on the whole a

democratic union. Its 3000 locals are nobody's property; they run their affairs as they see fit. On the national level the president is *primus inter pares*. The union is run efficiently and also democratically within the limitations imposed by the mass character of unionism.

The International Typographical Union is operated efficiently and democratically as regards relations between officers and members. The members of no other union so repeatedly rejected proposals by the officers to increase dues payments, and perhaps they erred in this respect. But the national leadership did not crush them, nor threaten to do so. Internal harmony was not disrupted. (And eventually the members voted the higher dues.)

To cite one more instance, the American Federation of Musicians in convention voted powers to their president, the late Herman Kenin (who succeeded Jimmie Caesar Petrillo), to dismiss the Federation's Executive Board and to write a new constitution for the union if and when he should deem this necessary. Efficiency is no less elastic a term than democracy; both change with time and circumstance.

The widely publicized disclosures of wrongdoing and abuse of power by the officers of some unions have evoked the rather widespread conviction that the "labor movement" is no more than a conglomeration of separate organizations that hold ceremonial conventions every so often to tell the world something that is not true. An increasing number of persons think that behind this facade each union is carrying on its own free private enterprise.

They are wrong. The well-publicized reports of Senate committees and the heavy emphasis in the press on the evil doings of some labor men tend to obscure the fact that they represent a minute fraction of labor leadership. The corruption-saturated climate in which the unions function has already been discussed. Labor is one of the cleaner movements in America.

What those disillusioned with labor tend to ignore is that quite apart from being an economic undertaking which each union pursues in its own way as an individual entity, unionism as a whole is also a cause and a faith which lend informal but vital authority to the power of organization. Faith, of course, is not easily defined; it has different meanings according to person and place.

Nor is morale a more accurate term with which to describe the set of beliefs that goes into the shaping of the behavior and consciousness of great numbers of unionists. Probably most workers are not clearly aware of these beliefs that nonetheless motivate them; and those who do consciously subscribe to a set of beliefs are not aware of them all the hours of their working lives. Yet these beliefs exist and are real and come powerfully alive in emergencies, whether evoked by leaders or in response to particular situations or provocative employers.

A generation ago, when it was not yet fashionable to be a bit cynical about labor, one of labor's most astute observers was the late Robert F. Hoxie. An academician who visited endless numbers of union meetings not to speak but to watch and listen, he wrote:

> The wage-worker's . . . hopes and fears center primarily . . . about the most vital concerns which immediately touch his present and future well-being—and the economic, ethical and juridical conditions, standards and forces that practically determine these matters; and his mind focuses on the problem of living as presented in these terms. In his attempt to comprehend and solve this problem he also develops some sort of social viewpoint—an interpretation of the social situation as viewed from the standpoint of his peculiar experiences and needs—and a set of beliefs concerning what should and can be done to better the situation, especially as it bears upon the conditions of living which he faces.[2]

In 1947, a quarter of a century later, Sumner H. Slichter, writing along similar lines, noted that a characteristically union-oriented way of thinking on many matters beyond pure-and-simple shop economics was gaining a hold on a community in which hired workers constituted the largest single segment. As the Slichter forecast of a "laboristic society" was too bold a projection for the days within sight, the Hoxie view comprised too little to indicate today's labor expectancies. But both scholars

accurately sensed the motivating drive that impels workers to join
up with the union and to become a power source through solidarity in action.

Millions have chanted the forever popular *Solidarity Forever*,
fervently feeling the words:

> When the union inspiration through the workers' blood
>   shall run,
> There can be no power greater anywhere beneath the sun.
> Yet what force on earth is weaker than the feeble strength
>   of one?
> Solidarity forever, Solidarity forever, Solidarity forever
> For the union makes us strong.

That power than which there can be "no greater anywhere beneath the sun" is the power of organization that unions develop
and accumulate. Obviously union power is not self-propelling. It
has to be encompassed, held, wielded, put to use. Organization is
the container of power, and leadership is its operating agent. But
all this is primarily rooted in the acceptance of union by the men
and women in the workplaces. In other words, the base of union
power is in the minds of the union members and they are therefore a most significant factor in the balance sheet of union power.

The old-time union operational mold has altered vastly in
the vastly altered circumstances in which unionists now work,
live and react to their own shop society and the social community.
The roles played by the local unions, national conventions, local
and national leadership and top officers have changed. The unions,
industry and the government have all grown big; and this bigness
must be lived with. The solution is not to endanger or diminish
democracy. What is called for is to create and learn to live with
big democracy.

The processing of justice by a competent, unbiased, outside
judicial mechanism is a necessity if democracy is to survive in
the unions. The town meeting "do-it-yourself" procedures no
longer fit the needs of modern democratic unionism.

The public discussion that preceded enactment of the 1959

labor reform law that was expected to protect democracy was based on two suppositions. One was that virtually all wrongs would be righted if union members were to participate fully in decision-making on all important matters. It was assumed that the members were democratically minded. The other supposition was that union leaders were anti-democratic. It was widely believed that once a union leader gets himself placed in office, he will be forever building power fences to defend his office.

There is certainly evidence to support the dark assumption about leaders, but there is evidence too to shake the cheering trust in the members' absolute dedication to democracy. Both members and leaders can be tempted at times to exploit opportunities and to indulge in wrongdoing for a consideration, just as can non-union-labeled men and women. But union members and leaders alike have amply demonstrated that loyalty to pledge and devotion to duty are not exceptions, but rather the overwhelming generality of union life.

In 1957 Professor John T. Dunlop wrote:

> The present challenge to labor unions is the development of new restraints and motivations within these organizations and their leadership. The challenge and necessity is a matter of their inner spirit.

The labor realities of the 1960s were a far cry from what they were just a few years earlier, in 1957; but for the 1970s internal democracy remains the key need of union life. Stronger restraints and motivations now challenge labor and demand more of the "inner spirit" which Dunlop stressed. Labor, like all of America, is in trouble, and will not overcome the trouble until it gathers new strength from within. From nowhere else can it come. If ever the union movement and the democratic process needed revitalization, it is now.

Power in the unions is inevitably centralized. The problem is to preserve the norms of ethical conduct in these mass organizations and to protect individual rights in circumstances which tend to reduce the individual member's significance and influence.

Nothing less will do than a challenging reactivization of the kind of fighting spirit that reinvigorated the moribund unions of the early 1930s.

The rise of white-collar workers to numerical dominance in the labor force need not be considered a hindrance to their being organized. As noted earlier, white-collar and other "middle-class" groups may prefer to form their own associations rather than to join a blue-collar federation.[3] That makes no difference in the long run. For they would be pursuing essentially similar objectives, unifying isolated workers and giving them strength and orientation. Parallel action by associations or union federations, by any name, would result in added strength for the whole labor movement. Internal union democracy would be strengthened by the force of expanding organization. And there are key common issues. Automation, for example, is no less a threat to white-collar workers than to the "blue" contingent of the work force.

Internal union democracy was not an issue when the unions led a full vigorous life in the mid-eighties of the last century and in the thirties and forties of this century. When there's a job to be done, union members generally do not stand on etiquette as to who does what; in such times the sense of being part of purposive doings fills the empty shell of merely "belonging." But the challenges of the '70s are shaping up in a nation which, since the mid-'60s, seems to have lost its sense of direction; the unions are part of the nation. Everybody is apparently waiting for somebody else to begin. The unions might as well make a start.

And this poses the most complicated question that union leadership has to answer, the fourth of the central queries raised earlier: Can leadership assure democratic functioning of the unions despite membership apathy or only limited participation in union affairs?

Since members' apathy is at times leader-made, and since bureaucratic or merely incompetent union administration can blight the interest of the members, a heavy responsibility devolves on the leaders. Early in this century, Daniel De Leon put this in a compelling sentence: "When you say organization, you say leadership." This is still true today.

As used by De Leon and also by this writer, the broad concept of leadership does not denote personal control of the union.

The leader of the huge contemporary union has many complex, difficult tasks. He must represent the members in negotiations with industry on terms of employment that no longer are limited to wages and hours. The specific business enterprise, at times the whole industry with which he deals, may be involved in or affected by the agreements he seeks. At the same time, the national economy and federal policies on domestic and foreign affairs are parts of the picture. The union leader must balance all these factors in what is always a delicate operation.

The union leader himself, in fact, is a business administrator, and the union itself is big business. Its collateral activities involve large responsibilities and the kind of big money that is inevitably attractive to racketeers, crooks, and embezzlers. Any going union with substantial financial reserves is likely prey, and any responsible labor leader must be aware of his union's vulnerability and take steps to insure its protection. Some of the most reputable unions in the country are currently engaged, *sotto voce*, in fighting off efforts by organized crime to muscle in on a good thing.

The union leader's function is also political. He must be able to induce multitudes of people to act in coordinated ways to pursue a variety of ends. And it is often a union leader's task to harmonize conflicting employers' interests in order to protect union interests.

In addition to bargaining, managerial, and political tasks, the union leader is a teacher, which should really be his supreme task. He may have at his disposal an education department and a public relations department. Useful as these may be, however, they do not perform that function which is solely his. The leader alone can impart to members the movement's "sense of the whole," convince them that the latter is indeed greater than the sum of its parts. He shares this rather difficult teaching function with others in the leader-echelon setup, provided he is leader enough to have the right kind of fellow leaders.

It has been said that union members get the leaders they deserve, even as nations do. Perhaps. But labor leaders, on the other hand, get the members that there are. They find and must live with them ready-made. The greater then is the task of leadership, to teach and lead the membership.

Under present economic and political circumstances, union

membership cohesion can no longer be maintained whole and holeproof by appeals to "duty," by symbolic gestures and rites, or by sentimental reminders of the old struggles "to build the union," although the traditional folklore still has a residual emotional potency. Some unions have faced up to the gap in member cohesiveness and are seeking to correct it by encouraging greater membership participation in decision-making. Other unions are merely developing educational and leisure-time gimmicks as substitutes for the depleted faith—with none too impressive results.

The relationship between the leaders and members is two-directional. Members can corrupt an honest leader by making unreasonable demands, by double-dealing, even as a dishonest leader can similarly injure the membership. This is a fact of union life that underlies the fifth and last question on internal union democracy: Can the abstractions of democracy and ethics in union codes be implemented by a floor under and a ceiling over the power of union leaders, to protect both leaders and members from wrongdoing by either to the other, or against acts inconsistent with union interests?

In some ways the 1959 labor reform act created such a floor under members' rights and a ceiling over the power of union leaders. But the legislation was not union-made and has little union acceptance. The inadequacies of the LMRDA already have been analyzed.

In the opinion of this writer, the forward strategy of protecting internal union democracy should include, in addition to safeguards in union constitutions, the following three reforms:

(1) *The establishment of an independent judicial process to review and compose internal conflicts.* As noted earlier, much could be accomplished by developing union-authorized machinery outside the unions to render binding decisions on internal conflicts. There is no evidence, however, to suggest that review boards like those of the UAW and the upholsterers' union have gained appreciable acceptance among union leaders. And, should this attitude ever be reversed, it would be exceedingly difficult to find enough persons with the requisite qualifications who could be induced to serve on the thousands of review boards that would have to be set up.

(2) *The protection of free expression of dissenting opinion*

at local meetings, at conventions and in union publications. Although some unions allow for such expression of opinion, many unions do not, as indicated by the Joel Seidman study cited earlier.

(3) *The development of specialized Courts of Intra-Union Relations as an implementation of the Bill of Members' Rights in the LMRDA.* This would help create a balance of members' democratic rights and leaders' authority.

Internal union democracy, however, needs more than protection in the courts. It needs intimate, understanding guidance by the national leadership. At present, local leaders are the force that keeps union democracy from being crushed by routine, selfish interests and external pressures. But not many of them have the ability, time, and power that the task demands.

Specialized Courts of Intra-Union Relations to exercise jurisdiction under Title I of the LMRDA would hold out one of the best hopes for fair settlement of disputes within a union. Such courts might well be patterned after family or domestic relations courts, as suggested in Chapter 3. It would require strenuous work by the best lawyers from relevant government agencies, interested public organizations, and the union movement to plan the courts properly. And it would then be a legislative task of no mean size to see the program through. Union leaders and their attorneys inevitably shy away from the prospect of more courts, whenever this is proposed.

The necessity to assure the internal democratic process is not an egghead daydream nor need it be a labor leader's nightmare. It is a reality by-product of our time of trouble. The combustive socio-political process that is moving into high gear cannot be avoided. The old internal power relationships are profoundly disturbed. Immense power came to many labor leaders almost overnight, often without much effort on their part, and that which heretofore never seemed to be a problem at all—the internal exercise of power—turned out to be a major headache. The fact is that in unions, as elsewhere, leaders rarely have insight into their own failings, particularly successful leaders. Success may be helpful to those who master it. But it destroys those who tend to become its slaves. Moreover, practicing unionists, leaders and those led, understandably have a limited interest in and at times only scant understanding of theories of democracy. But they usually are quick to grasp the potential implicit in any shifts of gravity in the pyramid of union power.

More than dutiful trips to the democratic drug chest for an annual dose of referendum voting and the like are required for the reconstruction of internal democracy to functioning health. And the health of the union movement is of crucial importance both to unionism and the pluralistic society of which it is part, whose very existence now requires that responsibility be widely distributed among individuals who function through integrated social forces. The 20,000,000 unionists organized in almost 100,000 organizations and delegated bodies, which in turn are part of some 200 national unions, apart from the over-all federations, constitute an enormous reservoir of social mobility. It would be the greatest disservice to open-end democratic society to immobilize these repositories of social energy by turning them into subunits of pure-and-simple bargaining agencies. The activization of the internal democratic process in the union movement is the command of the day.

8

THE RUBICON OF THE SEVENTIES

This volume has sought to focus on a few crucial areas that in sum are the measure of labor's internal power resources—of its capacity for democratic living and leadership in the testing days and decade ahead. In *Labor at the Rubicon* this writer has been searching, like many others, not only for the key to unionism's survival potential but for the ways in which it can contribute to the health of the whole society.

If internal union democracy—its difficulties, achievements, shortcomings and areas for proposed amelioration—has been stressed, along with the framework of pressures within which it functions, this is because without internal democracy, leadership can easily go astray, in the unions as anywhere else.

The union's internal democratic processes are the reins that help guide leadership in its immediate and long-range tasks. When these reins of democracy fall into disuse, or are too slackly held, the union leadership is understandably tempted to be moved by its own impulses or by whatever external drives and forces impinge on it most strongly. The way is then made easy for intervention into union affairs by government, management or even racketeers. Or the leadership itself may assume too dominating a role. Genuine democracy is accordingly essential not only for the members but for the leaders, for the union itself as a going enterprise, and ultimately for the nation too.

This in no way diminishes the all important role of leadership which is as essential to labor history as it is to human history. The statement that all of civilization rests on a dozen people may be exaggerated but it expresses a cogent truth and one that applies to unions.

As has been demonstrated in various labor situations analyzed earlier, leaders and members need each other; their interaction in the democratic process is labor's strongest defense. And although many people fail to realize it, also America's.

Abraham Lincoln, who was not a word waster, said it all when he remarked that "Workingmen are the basis of all governments."

A few of Lincoln's other comments about labor are worth recalling at this juncture:

Thank God we live in a country where the workingman has the right to strike.

Capital is the fruit of labor and would never have existed if labor had not existed first.

To secure to each laborer the whole product of his labor as nearly as possible is a worthy object of any good government.

Assuming the validity of Lincoln's view, so long as there is a free, democratic, constructive labor movement (despite scars of corruption and cupidity), the United States with all its faults (not excluding scars of corruption and cupidity) will remain free, democratic and constructive.

But when dictators rule, the unions and workers become their instruments. And tyrants historically have come to power most easily when citizens grow so careless of individual rights and democratic processes, either through hunger and depression, through apathy, or through fear in a situation of national anarchy, that the transition to autocracy can be made almost imperceptibly.

* * * *

Today warning voices are heard in the land, attacking the erosion of individual rights. But so long as the protests and demonstrations continue, freedom's bell will continue to ring out loud and clear in this most exceptional of nations—exceptional because never in its history has it been ruled by a king or dictator. This our modern Cassandras ignore; they also forget that since the mid-fifties several million Americans long deprived of full citizenship rights have had their first taste of freedom's flavor. And their appetites have been sparked.

America is a young country, a fact that will soon be underscored by its 200th birthday; unionism as a movement is perhaps 50 years younger, although some date its birth from 1792 when journeymen shoemakers in Philadelphia formed an organization which was the first continuing association of wage earners in America.

Of course the United States is already old and decadent in the view of most new African, mid-East, and Asian states struggling to assert or find a national identity. For most of these new states responsible self-government with participation in it by the citizenry and the development of the sense of belonging to a nation which one defends and is defended by is still a long way off. In the eyes—or propaganda machines—of the communist nations, too, America is on the decline.

There may be a truth in this distorted image of America, although the effort goes on to catch up with and surpass the idiotically wasteful but mightily productive U.S. economy. We are a young, vigorous nation—or were through World War II and the first innovative years of the post-war period. Will we in the '70s suddenly give way to age and all its debilities without ever having known the glories of mature, self-directed, conscious strength and purpose?

A 200th anniversary is a time for stock-taking. In this case it is more than that. By 1976 labor will no longer be able to evade the Rubicon that has been approaching with accelerating rapidity since midcentury.

The Rubicon that labor faces is no small stream such as separated Italy from Cisalpine Gaul. But labor must indeed determine whether or not to "take an irrevocable step toward a great objective"—as crossing the Rubicon has come to mean. Labor must decide, and soon, whether it will survive as a social force in democratic society.

A positive decision on labor's part is within the reality of

American life, within the social and economic power structure now in the disarray that precedes opportunity—or disaster. It is as if some far-off future has suddenly arrived. /

*   *   *   *

Over the run of history, oases of democracy evolved in one place or another but they were short-lived, few, and far between. These democratic enclaves existed in the most part for the well-to-do or educated elite; and they rested on slave bases, as in ancient Athens. The vast majority of Athenians were helots, slaves or near-slaves by any designation. Nor did Socrates, who questioned most things, ever question the system of slavery on which the good life was to be lived.

From the time of the Gracchi and the Spartacus-led rebellion, it took thousands of years for the movement to develop which changed the status of many slaves to indentured workers and then to free workers. The change came at different times for different groups in different lands and each had its own pace. It took centuries more and the Industrial Revolution before workers began to cohere into unions and still many years more for unions to regularize the employer-employee relationship through collective bargaining.

It was a long, bloody, often bitter battle, but one not without its moments of exhilaration, to reach the point where unionism stands today, the product not of anyone's theories but of many lives intensely lived.

Chief Justice Holmes understood and illuminated this area of the American experience as he did so many others. He stressed that the American Constitution is no static document but an ongoing "experiment." Of the Common Law he said: "The felt necessities of the time, the prevalent moral and political theories, intuitions of public policy, avowed or unconscious . . . have had a good deal more to do than the syllogism in determining the rules by which men shall be governed." [1]

These are words to remember at the brink of the Rubicon. The Rubicon which labor, with America, must cross now—or possibly never—is to respond with open, daring minds to "the felt necessities" whose adumbrations colored the '50s and '60s and whose reality will shake the world and labor with it long before the '70s end.

The anarchic forces of the 1960s are Thinking Big for the '70s. They include such seemingly disparate elements as the giant corporations, the political demagogues, the White Power and Black Power racists, the under-employed students flirting with Maoist revolutionary tactics, the remnants of student and other splinter leftist groups, as well as the quietly and skillfully organized rightists like the John Birch Society. There are a varied multitude of power-and-publicity-hungry individuals and groups spanning the political spectrum from left to right, all with an eye on "making it" in the '70s. They are part of labor's Rubicon.

A twelfth-century entry in the Polish-Lithuanian archives records that "The illustrious gentleman and knight, Michos Adrzievsky, stole a horse from the rascal and scoundrel, the Jew, Meyer Mendelson."

The case of labor in the high court of public opinion is not too unlike that of the "rascal and scoundrel" whose horse "the illustrious gentleman" appropriated. Perhaps the unions today are accepted as are the Jews, with the same unconscious qualifications among nice people; and with the same vicious bias among not-so-nice people. Innate anti-Semitism and the concept of labor as the slave of the state were skillfully manipulated in Nazi Germany with hideous effect, the Holocaust. The inherent antilaborism of conglomerate capital can be similarly manipulated. This is yet another facet of the Rubicon.

The history of labor has had its more limited and less spectacular tragedies than the holocaust of the Jews. But this difference matters little to a man killed in a mine blast due to continuing collusion of mine owners and government safety inspectors. To the victim's family, the resultant reality is terrible enough. To unemployed or suddenly disemployed workers, to migrant farmlaborers and their families, to the exploited women workers in Southern textile mills, to maimed mine workers who will never get jobs again and who know that their sons are doomed to dig coal underground as long as they are lucky enough to get work, despite the risk of lung cancer or of sudden death [2]—to these people, a private holocaust is here and now.

The engineer whose family sacrificed for his degree discovers that technology has made him superfluous. Recession strikes with sudden force at well-paid newsmen and other white-collar "intellectual" workers. Respectable middle-class school teachers unexpectedly find themselves going to jail because of injunctions against striking and picketing. Tens of thousands of Southern blacks, disemployed by cotton picking machinery and local politics, flood into Northern cities, where they lack rudimentary skills for even the most menial work (such as the ability to read an address or directions for using a cleansing fluid).

Each of these men and women, and with their children they number in the multimillions, lives in uncertainty, in poverty or on its awful borderlines. An oncoming depression—or "negative growth," the new, polite terminology—looms as a major threat for the 1970s if the Viet Nam war ever ends and an unplanned economy staggers into unplanned peacetime production. And if, on the other hand, the war continues and enlarges in scope, economic calamities will be compounded by increasing social disorders. This too is part of the Rubicon labor and America must cross.

Another crucial facet is the Government Snooping Establishment which grows ever vaster. The late and unlamented Senator Joe McCarthy would consider today's F.B.I. as indeed a monument to McCarthy's inquisition of the '50s . . . "I have here 205 names . . ."

Computers and acquiescence by the general public in now widely accepted procedures by which business as well as government and the military gather "information" about the most personal affairs and opinions of the citizenry have already resulted in immensely large data banks on the private thoughts and habits of millions, very possibly of most adult Americans. These dossiers of unverified data or, more accurately put, gossip, are easily stored and quickly accessible across the nation to parties unknown, invading by their very existence the constitutional right to privacy of Americans as never before. The technology for this massive destruction of privacy previously did not exist; the spirit unfortunately did. It has been routed before, and with determination can be extirpated again. This too, is part of the Rubicon.

The urban crisis which has been talked about for a decade is another central unresolved problem. About 75 percent of all

Americans are now concentrated in the cities and the trend out of the rural areas is continuing. Partly as a result of this and increasing unemployment, civil disorders in urban centers, now sporadic, may become a kind of permanent guerrilla warfare against symbols of authority. Urban blight and the crime-disease-death syndrome are tied closely to the disgraceful housing shortage. And the lack of decent dwellings is due in large part to the fact that real estate operators and construction companies put their money where the return rate is greenest fastest—into the construction of office buildings.

Rebuilding the cities is urgent, but building new housing is only a part of the answer. To rebuild the spirit of the city dweller is a still larger necessity. The alienation and loneliness of city dwellers are real; and are now immensely deepened by distrust and fear. It is the sense of community that is lacking. Much of the terror of urban life, aside from age-old greed and lust, comes from normal (and sometimes abnormal) unbuttoning of inhibitions in a locale where nobody knows anyone else. It always has been easier to get away with theft, murder and mayhem in a large metropolitan center than in a small town. So, as more and more of America becomes "metropolitanized" the crime figures go up. There are other factors, of course.

The fact that even the poorest slum dwellers have TVs and can see just how well the rich and middle-rich live, only a brief walk from their own rat infested, crumbling dwellings, is another inducement to crime. And when is a crime not a crime? For a hungry youngster to steal a loaf of bread and scoop up some other foodstuffs to bring home for the family, stealing may become part of a necessary survival pattern. For there is hunger in America, not only in rural slums but in the rich cities too. The polarization of wealth and poverty is central to the Rubicon.

TV itself is a factor in that fateful, upcoming event. Television has become the cultural bulldozer of our time (it need not be), appealing as it does, with the exception of Public Television, to the lowest common denominator. Children of rich and poor alike are exposed during their early, most impressionable years to the emotional and intellectual crippling induced by hours of gazing at the idiot box to which so many develop lifetime addictions.

It is nothing less than remarkable that the TV advertisements are always clearly photographed and projected to make their point. Not so the news. Sketchily presented, the rush of news becomes a hodge-podge of events so simplified or distorted by the speed of presentation that it makes no sense to the average TV watcher; and the sad fact is that it is through the TV that most Americans get what little information they have of world and national events. Since TV is with us to stay, the solution is more and better news coverage, not in occasional hour-long spectaculars on special subjects, many of which are excellent, but in regular, daily broadcasts that assume some intelligent interest in the eye and ear of the beholder. The influence of television is part of the coming Rubicon.

In the economic area, since 1959 the real Gross National Product has increased by 3.9 percent a year. According to the Bureau of Labor Statistics, labor productivity, that is output per man hour, in the private sector of the economy actually tripled between 1927 and 1967. But productivity growth in the private economy has since 1966 averaged only about 1.6 percent a year—and this at a time when the labor force has been increasing by over 2 percent annually.[3] Now the slow-down in the private economy (as yet unacknowledged by government or business) may be due partly to the increasing role of government on all levels as the nation's major employer and producer of services. But the more important factor is related to the trend of private industry to cut production at a point at which increased productivity brings the law of diminishing profits into operation—the point at which the more you sell the less you make. Hold-downs of this kind are inevitable in an economy whose primary thrust is the accumulation of capital.

These facts, viewed against the background of ever more rapidly advancing automation and computerization—and, finally, cybernation—convincingly tell us that one of the neglected necessities of the 1960s, which is a demand absolute of the 1970s, is a redefinition of work, job training, and retraining as a continuing life process. This, in turn, requires us to determine anew what is a living wage (for migrant farm workers as well as for doctors), how people will earn a living, and how those who cannot earn a living can live without destruction of their dignity, how people will spend their new leisure, participate in the community and in the accumulated knowledge of their time. All the vast information about the world we live in and the expanding worlds beyond the stratosphere do not make a culture or even contribute to one if it remains stored on tapes and is not part of the experience of the living.

A generation ago, Norbert Wiener, in his ground-breaking study of automatic controls and systems, pointed out that "There is no rate of pay at which a pick-and-shovel laborer can live which is low enough to compete with the work of a steamshovel." Automation especially affects unskilled labor, making inroads also into semiskilled, skilled, and even highly skilled occupations. Today middle-management people and white-collar workers are beginning to feel the computers breathing down their necks.

The cartoon showing a man turned down for a job despite front office approval "because the computer didn't like him" may be a slightly distorted portent of the future; and maybe not. In view of the routine use by some companies of computers in the hiring process and in view of the easily available dossiers on millions of Americans, it seems uncomfortably present and indicates a direction of proper union concern.

Opening up the dead-end economy and harnessing it and automation for human use is a large part of the Rubicon.

How does labor cross this Rubicon at which we have arrived and into which drain not only the accumulated ecological pollution of half a century, but also the sewage of 50 years of society's unsolved, festering social, political and economic problems? Does labor have the wherewithal to take them on, these enormous, complex problems?

The answer is yes, if. "If" relates to labor's putting its own house in order even as it undertakes the crossing of the Rubicon. These are parallel and mutually necessary tasks. Internal union democracy and its interrelation with leadership have been stressed throughout the pages of this book because they are the core of union power and of labor's capacity to use that power constructively on the social scene.

Internal democracy is critically important to labor for two reasons: it enriches the organization itself by developing and tapping the resources of the greatest possible number of individuals; and as noted earlier, it acts as a restraint on leadership and a guide to it. A union, no matter how great and good it may be, is in danger when it splits into a dichotomy of leaders and led. The key to achievement is in their interaction, their mutual interdependence.

Assuming then that labor seriously undertakes to strengthen internal union democracy, gearing its operations to great objectives as suggested earlier in this book, labor must then address itself to "the felt necessities" of the 1970s. This is a large order. It is part of the Rubicon labor must cross. It means enlarging the social focus, and this in turn means, among other activities, sponsoring plain down-to-earth literacy compaigns (illiteracy, virtually eradicated in the European countries, is still a problem in the United States). It also means greatly increasing on-the-job training and apprenticeship programs set up to wipe out once and for all discriminatory practices against Negroes, Puerto Ricans, Mexican Americans, American Indians, and other minorities struggling for entry into the economic system. And it requires going ahead full scale on programs of continuing workers' education and of upgrading skills to bring the unskilled, the suddenly disemployed skilled workers, and also many of the so-called unemployables into the economic mainstream. To date the government and the unions have only undertaken piddling efforts in this area and have had limited success. What is needed is a major effort that would achieve major results, enriching the lifeways of all economic groups and reversing the polarization which is dislocating all aspects of life in the nation. Disadvantaged groups must be given a strong assist up the job ladder or organized labor will, as noted earlier, soon pay a heavy price for neglecting this most searing of "felt necessities."

Not the least of these necessities is for the unions to face up to the problems not of organized and unorganized workers alone, but also to launch remedial action programs for and with the jobless, the unemployed, the disemployed, and for first-, second- and third-generation welfare recipients.

Admittedly the task is immense. But the whole history of unionism from colonial days when the bakers "conspired" to earn a living wage through the days of the East Side sweatshops, the Knights of Labor, the organization of mining, automobile, steel production, and all the other big industries, up to and including the unionization of teachers, of sanitationmen, of police and fire-men, of seamen and airplane pilots has been an immense task. Moreover, if the unions do not undertake to solve the problems of what might be described as the nonworkers, the government within the 1970s will be forced to do so because of growing dis-orders, quite apart from the problem of having a substantial—and increasing—sector of the citizenry subsisting on a dole, with the mischief-making potential of idleness or purposeless existence, a proclivity not at all restricted to the poor. And a Government solution to the problem of joblessness and welfare may be not at all to the liking or to the benefit of organized labor. The need for leadership in this area is so urgent and so widely—if vaguely—sensed, that the unions have only to start thinking and doing, to find willing helpers and associates, some of whom may well come from the young and compassionate.

So far as the institutionalized snooping activities cited earlier are concerned, labor would do well to launch an all-out attack on the practice wherever and whenever it occurs. Cessation of the maintenance and use of secret files could reasonably be a subject for collective bargaining, with the unions insisting that only per-sons directly engaged in national security activities be subject to F.B.I. or other types of clearance. Individual law suits backed by appropriate, directly concerned unions could be initiated—and should be—wherever there is a case of invasion of privacy or defamation of character. Law students and young lawyers could be enlisted in the effort to make snooping too costly a project for Government and private enterprise. In the process of fighting this battle, an important rapprochement might begin between the students and labor. This is an essential part of the Rubicon—call-ing a halt to established procedures for unwarranted and continu-ing invasions of individual privacy.

In another aspect of the Rubicon, housing, the first small steps have been taken. The Amalgamated Clothing Workers of America and the International Ladies Garment Workers Union have served as pioneers, one of their contributions being the construction of low-cost and middle-income housing for both union members and nonmembers. Their experience suggests that such housing can pay its way once graft and the grab for exor-bitant profits are eliminated.

Nor, apparently, are commercially-sponsored large scale housing projects entirely unprofitable. In any case The Metropolitan Life Insurance Company has, to date, shown no inclination to divest itself of the Peter Cooper, Stuyvesant Town, or Riverton developments; presumably upper middle-rent housing is economically feasible. These buildings were constructed years ago, but innovative methods, applying new factory mass-production techniques to housing construction, would greatly lower present costs. Conceivably the profit-hungry construction companies and the Luddite mentality of the construction unions might, with effort, be modified, and in fact replaced by policies of more enlightened self-interest. This, too, is an urgent necessity of our time.

It is true that, given the present state of the industry and the economy, low-rent housing is not financially possible without vastly increased federal and local aid. Labor has, of course, long promoted public housing programs; but it must now intensify its campaign for government-aided construction on a scale large enough to begin to replace our obsolete, inadequate, and socially destructive housing plant. Needless to say, the last vestiges of discrimination must be eliminated from the industry and from occupancy selection; color quota systems must go.

To date, union-sponsored housing has been along conventional structural lines. Labor, however, can certainly afford to experiment with prefabricated housing, which offers the only present prospect for rationalizing the building industry. A modern housing development in which factory-produced units are assembled, as they can be, speedily on a previously prepared site might serve as a useful demonstration project, paving the way for more general acceptance of modern, less costly construction methods. If several unions undertook such a joint cooperative effort, the result not inconceivably could help spur modernization of the construction industry. Just as union health centers, clinics, and medical care programs paved the way for Medicare and Medicaid, in housing also labor can do some urgently needed pioneering.

Not only can the unions do more themselves and push the building trades to undertake some overdue reformation of labor practices, but the unions can also enlist public support to improve existent housing and to provide associated amenities. Here again, students—in this case social science and urban affairs students as well as young architects and architectural students—are natural allies.

As indicated earlier, at least three-fourths of America lives in urban areas, an all-time high. The cities will soon be at the bursting point, with 90 percent of all Americans expected to move into the cities by the end of the 1970s. This is one of the facts of the new American way of life and a contributing factor to the tensions, crime and hazards of life in urban centers. Added to it is the unprecedented mobility characteristic of the second half of the century. Very few Americans live and die in the rural areas, towns or cities where they were born. The resulting loneliness of the cities, referred to earlier, is a continuing and worsening problem. The attempt to set up hippie communes is an intuitive answer, but not a solution to this widely felt necessity of our time for both community and security. (Student-labor cooperation here, as elsewhere, could be helpful in organizing meaningful neighborhood activities and cultural pursuits.) Some of the unions already conduct excellent educational and leisure-time programs for their members, which include concerts, lectures, art exhibits, and a wide assortment of courses; these might serve as nuclei for neighborhood-based programs—again, perhaps, with the cooperation of students and student organizations. And neighborhood-based citizen action could be mobilized by labor in a wide range of needed effort, from the provision of decent health care at reasonable prices and the setting up of day-care centers, to improved programming on commercial TV. In all of these areas, including medical care, the unions have wide experience which can be enlarged for community benefit—once the determination to move into the community is taken.

On a national level, basic restructuring is needed of our legislative system. The complexities and quickening rate of change in American life demand the creation of a Third House of Congress, as proposed in Chapter Two. This can no longer be delayed. And this too might well be a labor and student initiative, giving representation to the nation's varied economic and professional interest groups.

Straining to see beyond the 1970s, the mind blurs at the thought of the overproduction of toxins and trivia in which man may yet bury himself and all his works by the turn of the coming century. This is a fair possibility. But as a longtime devotee of the human species, and particularly of its workers, although not without appreciation of its untitled but authentic royalty like Holmes and Lincoln (who have more than once come to the rescue of this writer), and of the millions more, each unique, yet each carrying the recognizable spark of humanity—the people on whom civilization rests and always has rested—this observer, taking a long, hard, possibly last look at the human comedy, believes it will endure. And if it does, then it will go through what transmutations and to what glories none of us now living knows. All we do know is that we must, within the '70s, emerge at last from the cocoon in which we sleep.

The 1970s are the Rubicon, the watershed, not of labor history alone nor of American history alone, but of human development on planet earth. This is the decade in which we must decide once and for all time whether man will survive or will go down in the dunghill of his own making, in blind belief in "more," ever more, even when all proportion's gone in the vast dimensions of monstrous overgrowth.

Early in this century, at the start of that gigantism now threatening to annihilate the American social fabric, Booth Tarkington said in *The Turmoil:*

> And it was strong here as elsewhere—a spirit that had moved in the depths of the American soul . . . and emerged, tangible and monstrous, the god of all good American hearts—Bigness. . . . In the souls of the burghers there had always been the profound longing for size . . . We must grow! We must be big! We must be bigger! Bigness means money. . . . Their longing became a mighty will. . . . We must be bigger! Bigness means money! . . . Get people here! Coax them here! Bribe them! Swindle them into coming, if you must, but get them! Shout them into coming. Deafen them into coming! . . . We must be Bigger! Bellow to the Most High: Bigness is patriotism and honor! Bigness is love and life and happiness! Bigness is money! We want Bigness!

The road to Big Riches ended in rags, the Great Depression of 1929.

While the inflated gold rush ran its course to the abrupt stop, gold-diggers and patrioteers blustered and bluffed, and Murder, Inc. openly conducted its fatal business in the booze-saturated climate of lawlessness. Nonetheless intellectual life did not cease. To the contrary, Thorstein Veblen deeply probed the nature of the economic and political order—or disorder; Sinclair Lewis and Theodore Dreiser exposed the fatuity of the Babbitts and Elmer Gantrys, the titans and financiers of industry. Louis Vernon Parrington illuminated the potentials of America's cultural dynamics. John Dewey made his royal entry and his lasting contribution to social philosophy, even as Charles A. Beard and James Harvey Robinson cast searching light on the nation's history and promise.

On the national political scene, George W. Norris, Robert M. La Follette, Paul Douglas and Fiorello H. LaGuardia were gaining recognition and exerting a growing influence. A substantial socio-political progressivism was taking shape in the northern midwest. The Minnesota farmer-labor alliance was writing a new page in American history. It has not been erased. The unforgettable personalities of those years are not all gone; nor are they all forgotten. Of equally large and generous vision, America produced Franklin D. Roosevelt, Eleanor Roosevelt, Walter Reuther, Ralph Nader, Martin Luther King, Rosa Parks, John F. Kennedy and his brother Robert, and thousands more, some known, some unknown. Their ideas are holding things together and in the end may very well prevail.

When and if the nation produces the kind of leadership that can soberly assess "where we are and whither we are going," we will all know better how to get there. For lack of such national leadership, labor itself must assess the needs and get moving mentally to cross the Rubicon of the 1970s. When it does, millions will follow. For labor is, in the deepest sense, the people. It is America.

The ugly bigness of America described by Tarkington is still unfortunately a true portrait. But something has been left out. That is the largesse of America, its demonstrated ability to perform altruistically, and to organize itself, when the chips are down, for whatever job has to be done. Big, like black or white, can be beautiful.

There is little doubt in this writer's mind that today's turmoil will soon cast up the kind of daring, intellectually and morally big leaders that the people of America so desperately await.

These words are being written even as we arrive at that great crossing of worlds toward which all events since the 1950s have been hurrying us.

Historian Arthur Schlesinger Sr., in evaluating the ten most important events of the first half of this century, included the "upsurge of labor." Some future historian may not inconceivably rate among the most important events of the second half of the century "labor's innovative action in mobilizing America for democracy." That page remains to be written.

The hour is late. Far too late for hesitation. Much too early for despair. We stand at the Rubicon. If we are to continue the great experiment that began with the Constitution almost two hundred years ago, "We, the people . . ." had better get moving.

POSTSCRIPTS

What I Have Learned

I would not lay claim that I have learned too much for comfort but I will assert two positive aspects of the learning process:

1. I learned a good deal from books, having been a voracious reader from early years on: information and generalizations. But I learned incomparably more from life, that is from people, and observing their ways of living together, or against one another, or group-wise, and from dealing with them.

2. And I learned to unlearn. Ideas, value judgments, orientations tend to stay put, acquire a seniority right. But to continue valid, they need frequent intellectual ventilation. Indeed, an old Russian saying hints at it: "Live long, forever learn, die a fool." Guarding against hardening of intellectual arteries was necessary in the good old days when life and living seemed to be possessed of a modicum of permanence, and ability to unlearn was protection against "dying a fool."

Looking at life in 1968 from the vantage point of age 85 and back, examining 70 years of aware observation and participation, the experience now appears as having been anything but smooth, steady, consistent. And it never was. Nineteen hundred sixty-eight is a year of uncertainties, of crises, of revolution, the *r* in lower case. But no different were most of the years of the anxious decades and their predecessors. Only that most of us felt that we were attempting to bring history into motion, to change a static reality, the truth having been that reality was constant change and not infrequently we resisted, blocked big changes by persistence on small changes. Ability to unlearn, at times rather slowly, was perhaps a saving grace.

Notes

Chapter 1

1. In August 1969, miners' pension payments, then 115 dollars per month, were increased to 150 dollars. In 1961 they had been cut from 100 to 75 dollars due to lowered production; in 1965 there was an increase to 85 dollars and in 1967 an increase to 115 dollars a month.

Average pay for bituminous coal miners was five dollars and seventy cents an hour in 1969, an increase of almost 50 percent (4.5 percent a year) over hourly pay in 1960, according to the Department of Labor's Bureau of Labor Statistics. The Bureau said that employer expenditures for retirement programs accounted for 15 percent of the rise in compensation. In the period 1960-1969, monthly benefits and the number of pensioners increased. During this period also, a 35 percent increase in coal production was reflected in increased payments by mine operators to the Welfare and Retirement Fund. In 1969 employer outlays for retirement programs represented 11.1 percent of compensation; employer outlays for health and insurance programs were 8.5 percent of compensation.

In 1971, twenty-five years after the miners' Welfare and Retirement Fund was set up, the Fund said it had distributed over three billion dollars in benefits to miners and their families. The Fund reported that 141,520 miners had received pensions and that half a million persons had been reached by the medical and hospital care program in the 25 years. Some 67,000 miners are now drawing pensions.

2. The Senate Select Committee to Investigate Improper Practices in Labor or Management, John L. McClellan, Chairman.

3. Americans are now spending 105 billion dollars annually for leisure and recreation, according to *U.S. News & World*

Report, issue of April 17, 1972, which forecast that the leisure boom will more than double in the seventies. A feature article, "Leisure Boom: Biggest Ever and Still Growing," said that expenditures for recreation and leisure time activities exceed national defense costs.

4. Unemployment rose to 5.9 percent in 1971 and over the first five months of 1972 hovered around a 5.9 percent high with over five million unemployed.

5. Nearly 47,000 of New York City's 59,000 teachers struck the schools on September 9, 1968 in the first of three strikes during that year, interrupting the education of 1.1 million children. On May 15, 1970, Albert Shanker began a 14-day jail term for having led the 1968 strikes. A $220,000 fine was levied against the union.

6. White-collar membership in unions totaled 3.4 million in 1970, according to the Bureau of Labor Statistics. This was an increase of 177,000 from 1968. Total union membership was 20.7 million in 1970.

In its first membership survey covering public and professional employee associations together with labor unions, the Bureau noted that the former "have grown substantially in recent years."

Public employee unions have become the fastest growing segment of labor. The American Federation of State, County and Municipal Employees (AFSCME), with almost 450,000 members, is now about the 12th largest union in the country; its membership went up 112 percent between 1960 and 1970. The American Federation of Government Employees (AFGE), with almost one-third of a million members, had a growth of 362 percent between 1960 and 1970. The American Federation of Teachers went from 56,200 members in 1960 to 205,300 in 1970, an increase of 265 percent.

As of 1968, white-collar workers accounted for only 16 percent of all union members, on the basis of a survey by the National Industrial Conference Board, released in July, 1970. The NICB study, entitled "White Collar Unionization," showed an increase of only 1.0 million white-collar union members between 1958 and 1968.

Chapter 2

1. Government figures show that about 16 million American families have annual earnings of under 7000 dollars a year. This is

almost one out of three families; and in some there are two wage
earners. There are 51,948,000 families in the United States; the 16
million who live on less than 7000 a year represent 31 percent of
that total.

Annual Family Income	Number of Families	Percent of Families in 1970
under $3000	4,601,000	8.9
$3000-$5000	5,341,000	10.3
$5000-$7000	6,148,000	11.8

The total number of families represented in the table that
make less than 7000 dollars annually is 16,090,000. A family of
four living in a big city can barely subsist on 7000 dollars a year.

An additional 12,046,000 persons who are not part of a family
unit also earn under 7000 dollars per year. For them as well, life
is not easy. There are 15,357,000 non-family persons in the United
States.

Annual income of Unrelated Individuals	Number of Individuals	Percent of Unrelated Individuals in 1970
under $3000	7,453,000	48.5
$3000-$5000	2,720,000	17.7
$5000-$7000	1,873,000	12.2

Less than $1500 is nowhere near a living income. Nor can
even single persons and those living on the land and raising some
of their own food enjoy a modicum of comfort on "under $3000."
In the cities "under $5000" is poverty.

While wages have gone up, living costs have erased earnings
gains. Thus, between 1960 and 1970, the cost of living, as measured by the Consumer Price Index, increased 31.1 percent, with
a marked acceleration beginning in 1966.

Since 1950 the purchasing power of the dollar has declined
by 38 percent.

During the same period, output per man hour in the total

166   LABOR AT THE RUBICON

private economy increased from 59.7 in 1950 to 104.3 in 1970 (1967=100).

In 1967, net spendable earnings (average gross weekly earnings less social security and income taxes) were $90.86 for a worker with three dependents in the private nonagricultural sector of the economy. In 1969, net spendable earnings rose to $99.99, but after adjusting for increases in consumer prices over the two-year period, "real" net spendable earnings were $91.07 in terms of the purchasing power of the 1967 dollar. A rise in spendable earnings to $104.61 in 1970 was equivalent to only $89.95 in terms of the 1967 dollar. Thus between 1967 and 1970 there was a decline in real earnings, based on the purchasing power of the 1967 dollar.

2. The proposal for a House of Functional Representatives was first set forth by J. B. S. Hardman in *Labor and Nation*, October, 1945 and in *Mature Collective Bargaining: Prospects and Problems*, Institute of Industrial Relations, University of California, 1952.

3. "Industrialism and World Society," by Clark Kerr, John T. Dunlop, Frederick Harbison and Charles A. Myers, *Harvard Business Review*, January-February 1961.

Chapter 3

1. The Secretary of Labor instituted 35 court actions in Federal district courts challenging union elections during fiscal 1971. As of June 30, 1971, a total of 246 cases had been filed in civil suits under Title IV in the 12 years since the LMRDA went into effect.

In fiscal 1971, there were 132 complaints of election irregularities received and investigated; 35 elections were supervised pursuant to court order. Another 20 cases were closed through voluntary compliance, including supervised and unsupervised rerun elections.

Under Title I, approximately 30 private civil actions were brought in district courts of the United States by union members for alleged violation of members rights during fiscal 1971.

2. In May, 1972, two and a half years and three murders after the December 1969 election of United Mine Workers President W. A. (Tony) Boyle, his election was declared null and void by a United States District Court. Judge William Bryant, in a 33-

page decision, found evidence of wrongdoing in the campaign and at the polls "too strong to resist."

This was the first time since enactment of the LMRDA, known as the Landrum Griffin Act, that its provisions had been implemented to overturn a major union election on a national level.

The 1969 U.M.W. election pitted incumbent President Tony Boyle (personally selected by John L. Lewis as his successor) against an insurgent slate headed by Joseph A. Yablonski. Three weeks later Yablonski, his wife and daughter were slain in their home in Clarksville, Pennsylvania. (A grand jury returned a series of Federal indictments against several union officials in connection with the slaying; and on May 10, 1972, the U.M.W. president was questioned by the same grand jury in response not to a subpoena—after all he is a union president—but to what United States Attorney Richard A. Thornburgh described as an "invitation." Boyle was accompanied by his attorney. Also "invited" to answer questions on the same day were Boyle's executive assistant, the union's assistant secretary-treasurer and the president of District 19. The union's financial records and correspondence between national headquarters and District 19 in Kentucky and Tennessee had already been subpoenaed and were in the hands of the grand jury. Richard A. Sprague, special prosecutor for the state of Pennsylvania, said District 19's Research and Information Fund was a "murder fund," that its money came from national headquarters and was used to pay Yablonski's killers. Three persons have pleaded guilty and two have already been convicted and sentenced to death in the murders. As of late May, 1972, action on two others linked to the killings was pending.)

Official results of the 1969 election, were 80,577 votes for Boyle and 46,073 for Yablonski; it was the first real challenge to the union's leadership in 43 years.

Election complaints filed with the Department of Labor under the LMRDA accused the union of corruption and charged its president with being a "dictator" and "embezzler." These charges were ignored until after Yablonski's death. Early in 1970, soon after the Labor Department began investigating the charges, its general counsel rather prematurely said that the election had been conducted "with the highest degree of honesty and integrity."

Finally, however, the Department, in accordance with LMRDA regulations, moved to file a civil suit, asking that the election be voided and new elections ordered under the department's supervision.

A six-month trial ensued. (While it was in progress Boyle was convicted in the Washington D.C. Federal District Court on 13 charges of conspiracy and of illegally using union funds to make political contributions—a conviction that could result in up to 32 years in jail and a $120,000 fine.)

At the end of Boyle's half-year trial on election fraud charges, Judge Bryant cited a series of violations of Federal law by the leadership, including improper use of the union newspaper to promote Boyle's candidacy, improper campaign expenditures and lack of adequate safeguards to insure a fair election.

Of course similar violations routinely occur—with notable exceptions—in the election proceedings of almost any big union. In this case, however, it was the murder of the opposition leader and his wife and daughter, together with the insistence of his two surviving sons, and the brilliant work and persistence of a skilled lawyer, Joseph L. Rauh, Jr., that finally forced the issue despite Labor Department reluctance.

Judge Bryant's carefully documented opinion noted that the mineworkers' official publication "was used as a campaign instrument for the incumbents," pointing out that in five issues there were 166 references to Boyle and a virtual blackout on the Yablonski slate of insurgent candidates. Again, anyone familiar with the labor press knows that the mineworkers' journal was not unique in its fulsome praise for the leader and denial of space to the opposition, but was merely following prevailing custom.

Judge Bryant further found that Yablonski's removal from the union's executive board (of which he had been a member prior to his candidacy) was "a direct reprisal for his running for president."

Additionally, the judge said that in a great number of the locals, "little regard was shown for the . . . secret ballot," one of the requirements under Title IV of the Labor Management Reporting and Disclosure Act of 1959.

The judicial opinion was that these and other findings constituted a violation of the LMRDA.

Meanwhile, Miners for Democracy, an organization of Ya-blonski dissidents, nominated candidates to oppose Boyle and other top officers in federally supervised rerun elections.

The late Mr. Yablonski's sons, on May 4, 1972, charged the Labor Department and former Secretary George P. Shultz with long "failure to heed" their slain father's requests to investigate the UMW.

All of this underscores the need to amend the 12-year old LMRDA, making it a more genuine instrument for safeguarding internal union democracy.

Chapter 6

1. Bureau of Labor Statistics, U.S. Department of Labor, December 1960.

2. *U.S. News & World Report*, November 2, 1959.

3. *John Herling's Labor Letter*, June 5, 1965.

Chapter 7

1. "Political Controls and Member Rights: An Analysis of Union Constitutions," by Dr. Joel Seidman in *Essays on Industrial Relations Research Problems and Prospects*, Institute of Labor and Industrial Relations of the University of Michigan and Wayne State University, 1961.

2. *Trade Unionism in the United States*, 2nd ed., Appleton-Century-Crofts, New York, 1923.

Chapter 8

1. *The Common Law* by Oliver Wendell Holmes Jr., 1881, in *Readings in Jurisprudence and Legal Philosophy* by Morris R. Cohen & Felix S. Cohen, New York, Prentice Hall, 1951.

2. On May 2, 1972, a flash fire in the Sunshine silver mine in Kellogg, Idaho, killed 91 miners. The bodies of the last victims were brought out ten days later, after which efforts were begun to seal off the fire area. *The New York Times* reported that Marvin C. Chase, general manager of the mine, which is the richest and deepest in the nation, said he believed the fire began by spontaneous combustion. The Steelworkers union said the catastrophe was due to the Sunshine Mining Company's "callous disregard" for safety.

Frank McKee, western district director of the Steelworkers, demanded that responsibility for mine safety be taken away from the Bureau of Mines and turned over to the Labor Department.

In testimony before the House Labor Committee, Mr. McKee charged the company with failure to install an adequate fire warning system and to train employees on how to escape in case of fire. He said that the company had not complied with a law requiring that there be two ways out of the mine and that there were no alternate escape ways from the bottom 600 feet of the mine. (The mine is a mile deep.)

Noting that the elevator operators lacked self-rescue chemical masks, the union official said: "When they died, the elevators stopped running since they were impossible to operate from above ground."

Union officials scored the Bureau of Mines for "coddling" the mining industry and softening safety standards under pressure from industry lobbyists. The comment of mineworker Keith Collins was: "There ain't no such thing as a safe mine. It's like walking in front of a truck and saying it's safe because the truck didn't hit you."

3. The Gross National Product was 475 billion nine hundred million dollars (475.9) in 1959, in terms of the 1958 dollar. According to the U.S. Bureau of Commerce there was steady increase in the next decade to a then record high GNP of 727 billion five hundred million dollars (727.5) in 1969. Then came a decline. In 1970 the GNP fell to 724 billion one hundred million dollars (724.1).

Despite the Administration's hopeful forecasts, realistic indications such as continuing inflation, high unemployment, and engineered under-production in order to swell profits, suggest lags in GNP growth during 1971 and 1972 similar to 1970.

Herbert Stein, Chairman of President Nixon's Council of Economic Advisers (CEA), however, thinks otherwise. In an article, appropriately entitled "Things Look Better," published in *The New York Times* on March 21, 1972, he forecast that "the Gross National Product would rise by about $100 billion in 1972," reaffirming the prediction in the CEA's January economic report. In Stein's article there was no indication of whether the anticipated 100 billion dollar GNP increase was in constant dollars, having reference only to goods and services produced (as in the GNP totals cited above) or whether it also included inflated prices for them.

Backing up this estimate which, in terms of real dollars, seems rather overly optimistic, the President's chief economic adviser argued that economic developments since the start of 1972 indicate that the year will be one "of rising production, declining unemployment and a lower rate of inflation."

Mr. Stein assumed that the unemployment rate would decline to 5 percent by year's end, and that the administration would succeed in achieving an inflation ceiling below 2 to 3 percent by December 31, 1972.

As to unemployment, Mr. Stein noted a decline from 6 percent in December 1971 to 5.7 percent in February, but warned that "this two-month decline of 0.3 per cent is a faster rate of decline than we expect for the year as a whole."

According to many union research departments, unemployment in May 1972 was at least 6 percent; and in some cities it was much higher.

During the 1968 election campaign, President Nixon indicated that a little unemployment might be a good thing. Nothing he has done in the Presidency suggests that he has since changed his mind.

Mr. Stein's rosy view of the economy may make interesting reading in 1973. But in the spring of 1972 the Stein forecasts were not unique. Dr. Walter Heller, now a professor at the University of Minnesota and previously Chairman of the Council of Economic Advisers under Presidents Johnson and Kennedy, on May 17, 1972 said he thought the economy was "moving up" vigorously. He predicted a further upward revision, by June 1st, of the GNP. While Dr. Heller expressed the view that the outlook for profits was "quite favorable," he said that unemployment was "most stubborn" and would be "very slow" in going down. However, like Mr. Stein, he also predicted a drop in unemployment in 1972.

In contrast to the Stein and Heller statements, an item in *Steel Labor*, official publication of the Steelworkers union, in its January 1972 issue said: ". . . the Labor Department reported that the U.S. wound up 1971 with the highest unemployment in twelve years: 65 major areas reported six percent or more unemployed."

On profits the news was more cheerful. *U.S. News & World*

Report, in its issue of April 24, 1972, said that combined profits of the nation's 25 leading manufacturing companies increased 28 percent in 1971 and that the first quarter of 1972 indicated that the upward surge would continue.

General Motors alone showed a profit increase of 218 percent to 1936 billion dollars in 1971. Standard Oil was number two, with profits up 16 percent and totalling 1517 billion dollars. IBM was the third largest earner, with just under 1100 billion dollars, a profit increase of 6 percent.

The same issue of *U.S. News & World Report* showed that unemployment was 9 percent or more in the Seattle area and that it was from 6 to 8.9 percent in Oklahoma City, St. Louis, Wichita, Fresno, the Los Angeles area, Portland, and San Diego. The over-all picture was described as "moderate," with unemployment ranging from 3 to 5.9 percent. Basic data used was from the U.S. Departments of Labor and Commerce.

By the summer of 1972 there was good news from Washington: unemployment had dropped to 5.5 percent in June; median family income for 1971 had reached an all-time high of 10,285 dollars, up 418 dollars from 1970. But the gain was in fact cancelled out by inflation.

The Commerce and Labor Departments on July 21 reported that the real GNP (discounting inflation) rose at an annual rate of 8.9 percent in the second quarter of 1972. The nation's total output of goods and services reached a rate of 1,139 billion dollars a year in the April through June period, an increase of 30 billion over the first quarter.

Although the figures were preliminary, the Commerce Department described the growth rate as "prodigious."

Herbert Stein, whose earlier predictions were thus confirmed, said the Government reports were "the best combination of economic news to be released on one day in a decade."

The headline of the front page lead story in *The New York Times* read: "Gain in Economy Fastest Since '65; Price Rise Slows."

"Despite higher food prices," said *The Times,* "the Consumer Price Index rose by only two-tenths of 1 percent over the May figure, or one-tenth after adjusting for normal seasonal changes in some prices."

Instead of the 3 percent annual inflation that had been standard since 1967, the rate was 2.9 percent in June 1972.

New York Times columnist James Reston was not impressed.
On July 23, two days after the good economic news broke, his
comment was: "Unemployment and prices are still very high.
People out of work are more interested in jobs and the actual
price of meat than they are in the *rate* of unemployment and the
rate of the price rise of groceries in the second quarter of 1972.
The fact is that food prices went up, and, on the whole, jobs for
unemployed and underemployed went down, and for families in
trouble, this is more important than the trends of the gross national
product or the graphs of the Consumer Price Index, 'seasonally
adjusted.' "

Among "families in trouble" were 25.6 million persons who
live in poverty according to Census Bureau estimates for 1971. The
total for 1970 was 25.4 million. The Census Bureau said the
200,000 increase was statistically insignificant, falling well within
an estimated sampling error. The official poverty line now is 4,137
dollars for an urban family of four; it was 3,968 dollars in 1971.

The Census Bureau's latest poverty total (released in July
1972) is the highest since 1967 and represents 13 percent of the
nation's families. Among whites, 10 percent are poor; among
blacks, 31 percent are poor.

The gap between rich and poor almost doubled in the 20
years between 1949 and 1969. A study released by the Joint Economic Committee of Congress in March of 1972 pointed out that
whereas the real income gap between the richest 20 percent and
the poorest 20 percent of all families in the United States was
10,565 dollars in 1949, it was 19,071 dollars in 1969. The study,
prepared by Professors Lester C. Thurow and Robert E. B. Lucas
of the Massachusetts Institute of Technology, notes that although
average incomes are rising, "the distribution of income around this
average is not changing." The authors set forth a series of innovative proposals to achieve such change.